Canadian Rocky Mountain Scenes

Canadian Rocky Mountain Scenes

With 52 Quotes from the Book "Considering Wisdom"

Elfriede Copple

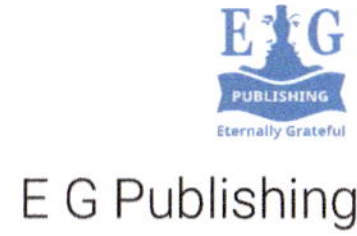

E G Publishing

CONTENTS

1 | Wisdom versus Knowledge — 1

2 | Common Sense of Wisdom — 5

3 | Consider the Source — 9

4 | Admit and Repent — 11

5 | In Pursuit of Wisdom — 19

6 | Wisdom Found by Listening — 25

7 | Wisdom in Voting — 31

8 | Unforeseen Future — 38

9 | Forgive and Forget — 41

10 | Spiritual Warfare — 43

11 | Delicate Issue — 45

12 | Unrevised History — 49

ABOUT US — 55

CONTENTS

BOOKS BY MICHAEL COPPLE   57

Wisdom versus Knowledge

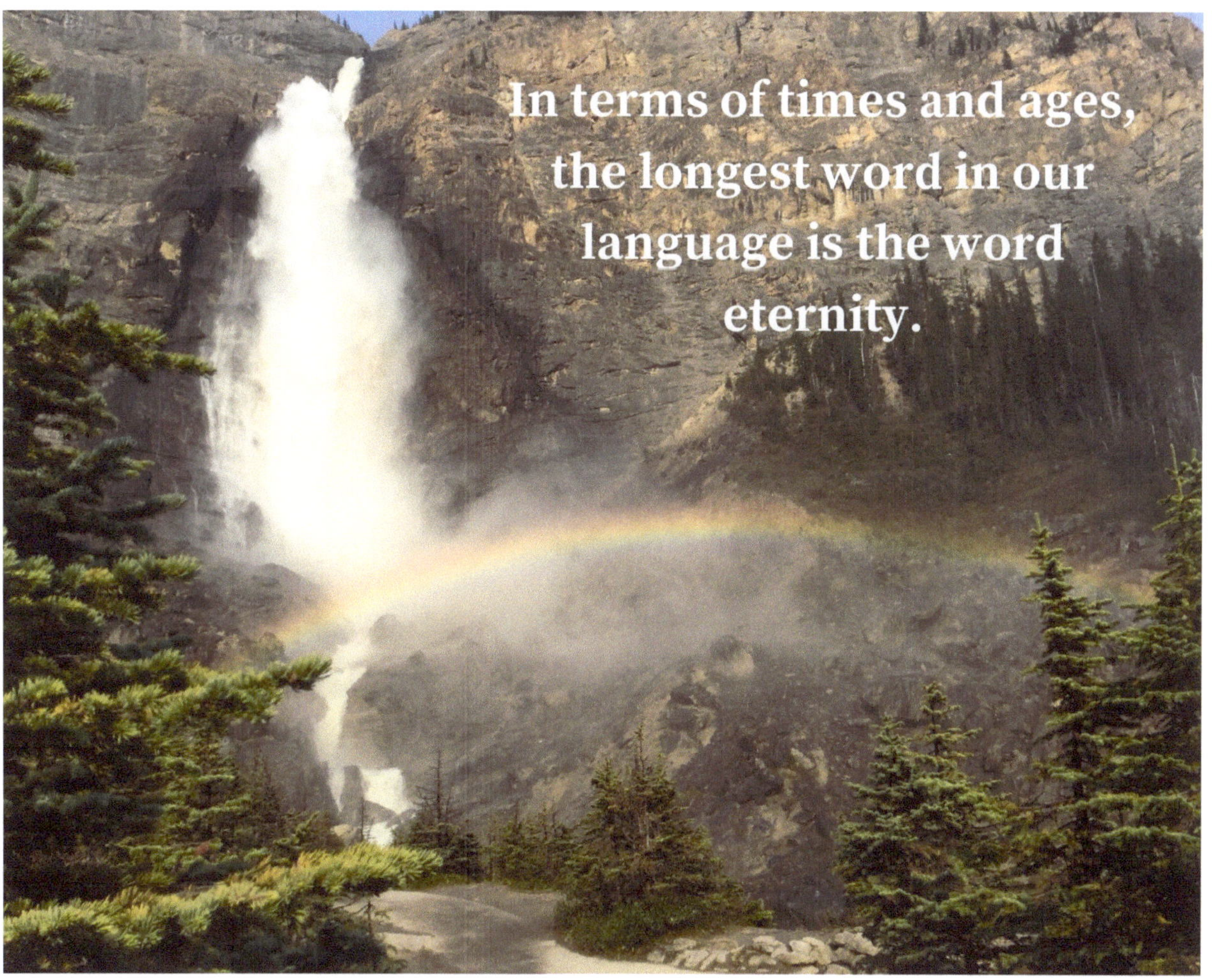

Takkakaw Falls - Yoho National Park - British Columbia

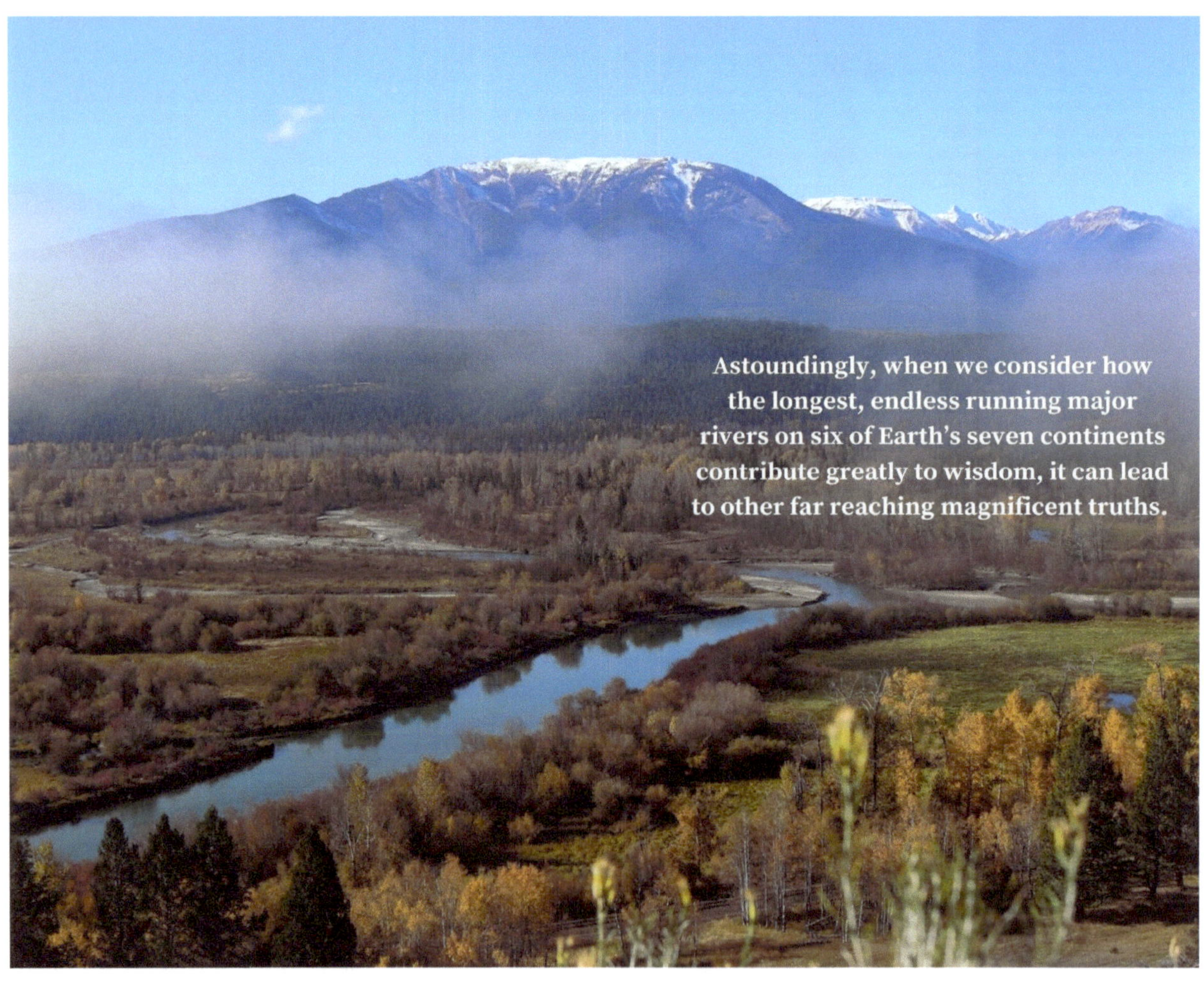

Old Coach Trail – Columbia River – Invermere – British Columbia

The mountains were formed on the fourth day of creation, but the flood did not occur until sixteen hundred and fifty years later. The fish fossils that were created on the fifth day, being found on Mount Everest, provide clear evidence that the earth was totally under water.

Fire Tower Lookout – Susan Lake – Columbia Valley – British Columbia

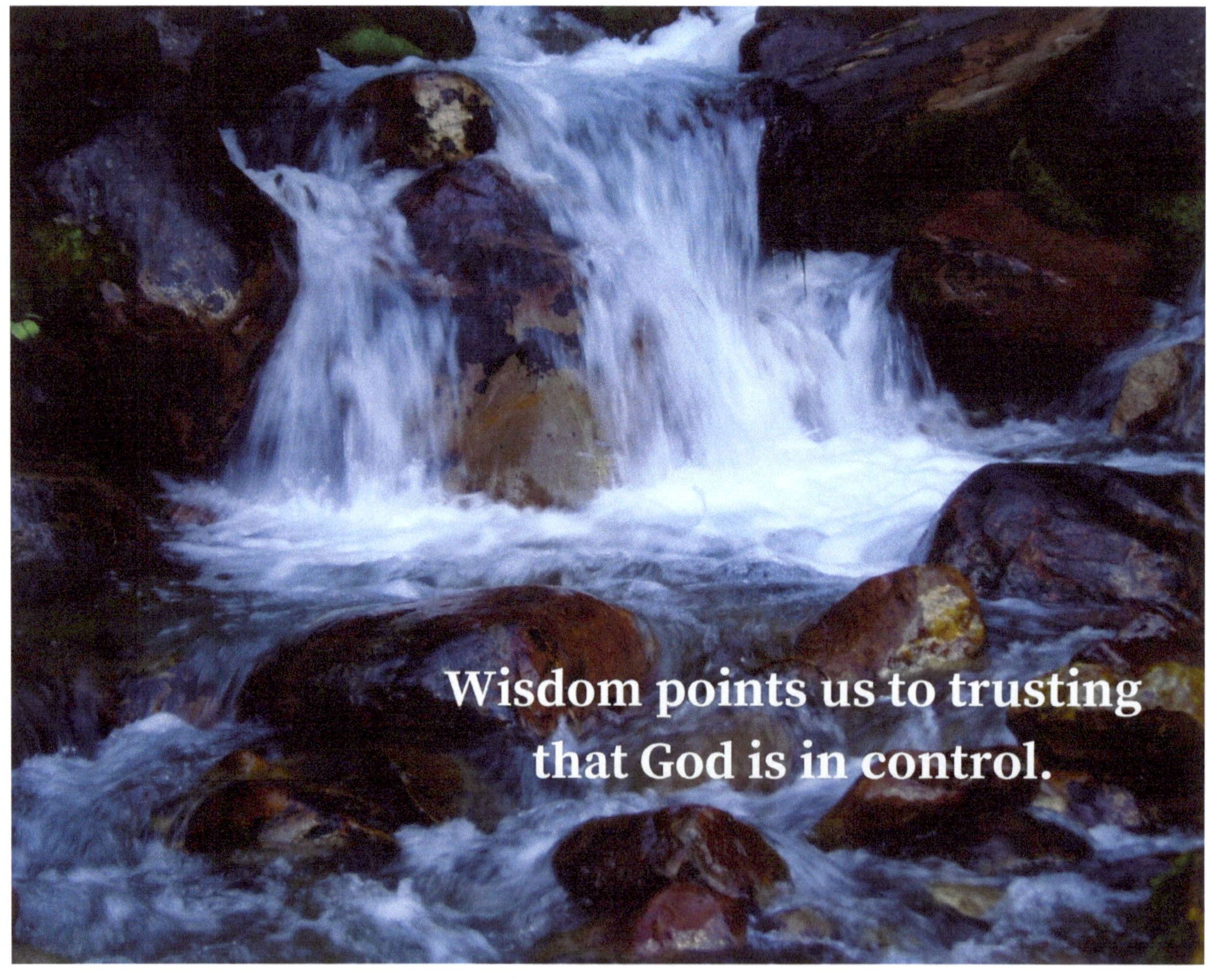

Quarz Creek Trail – Columbia Valley – British Columbia

Common Sense of Wisdom

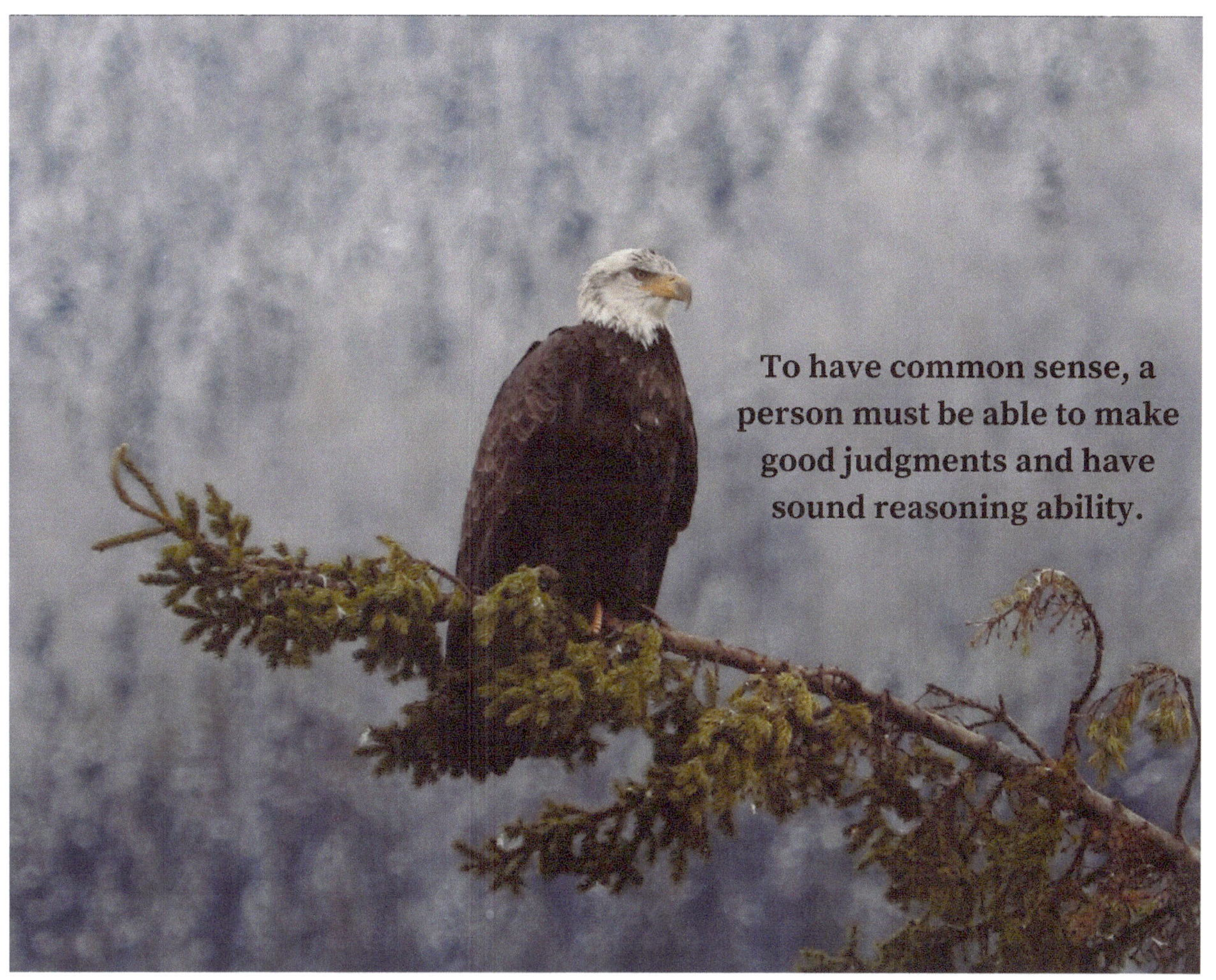

Bald Eagle – Blaeberry River – Blaeberry Valley – British Columbia

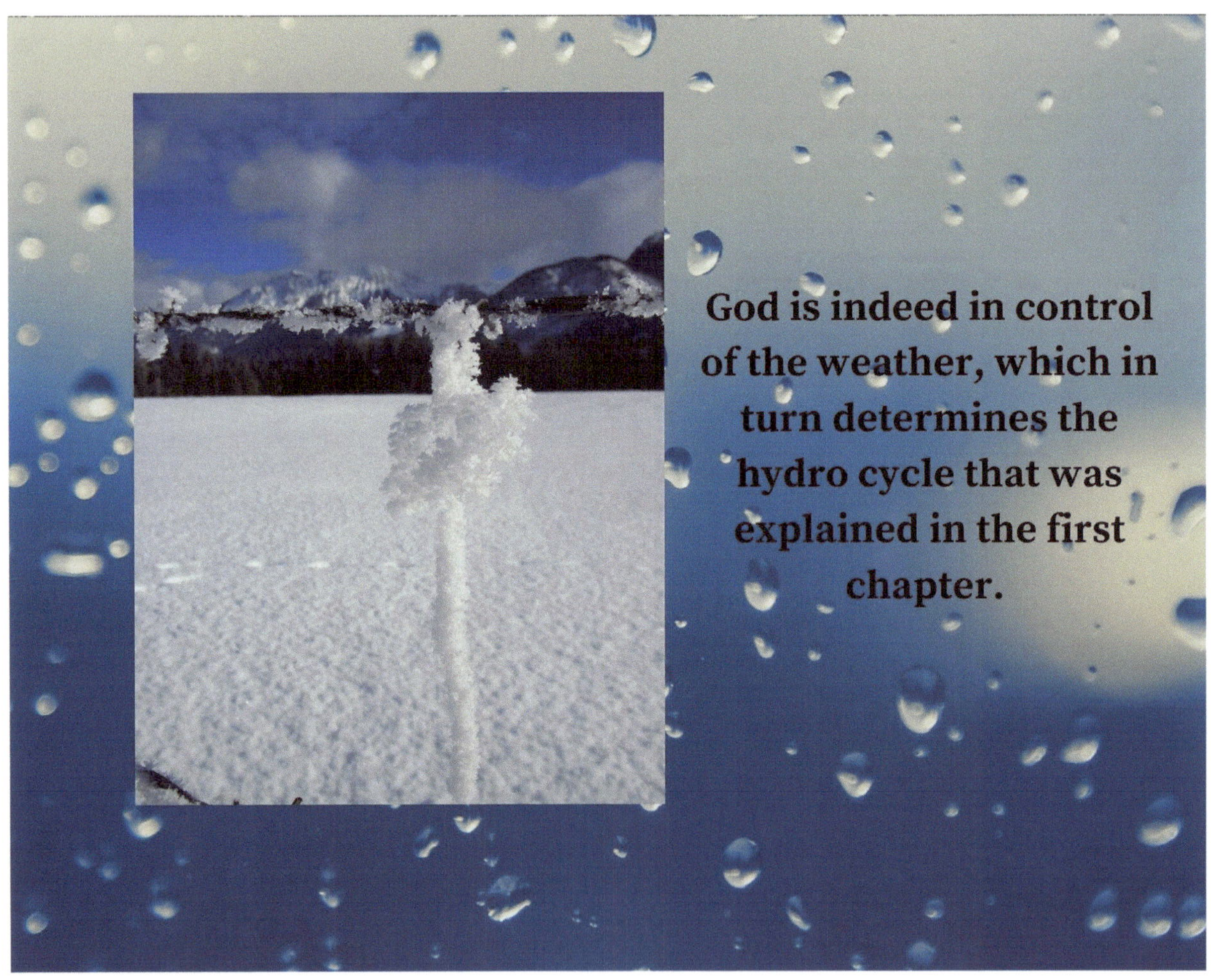

Snow Cross attached to Barbed Wire Fence – Blaeberry Valley – British Columbia

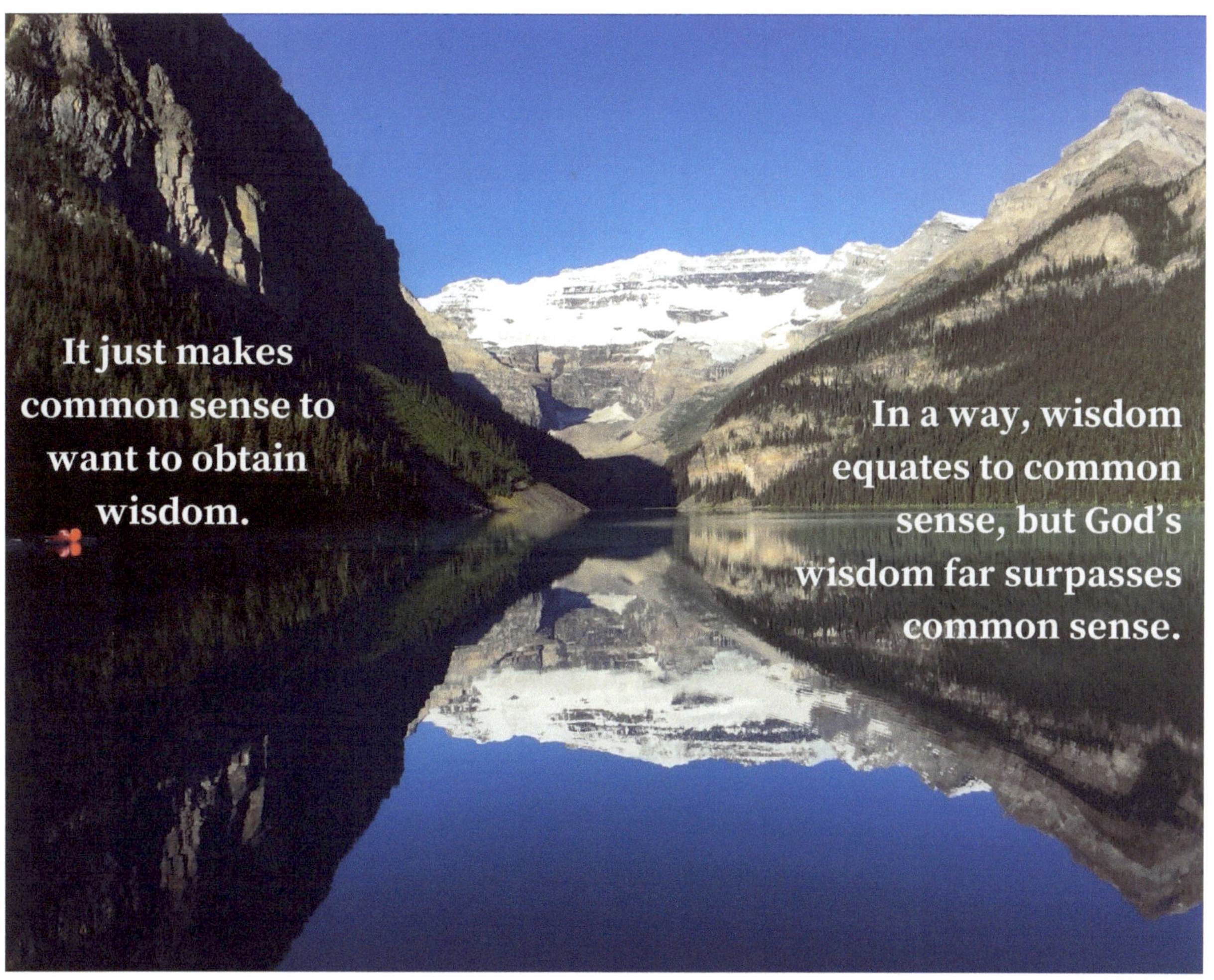

Lake Louise – Banff National Park – Alberta

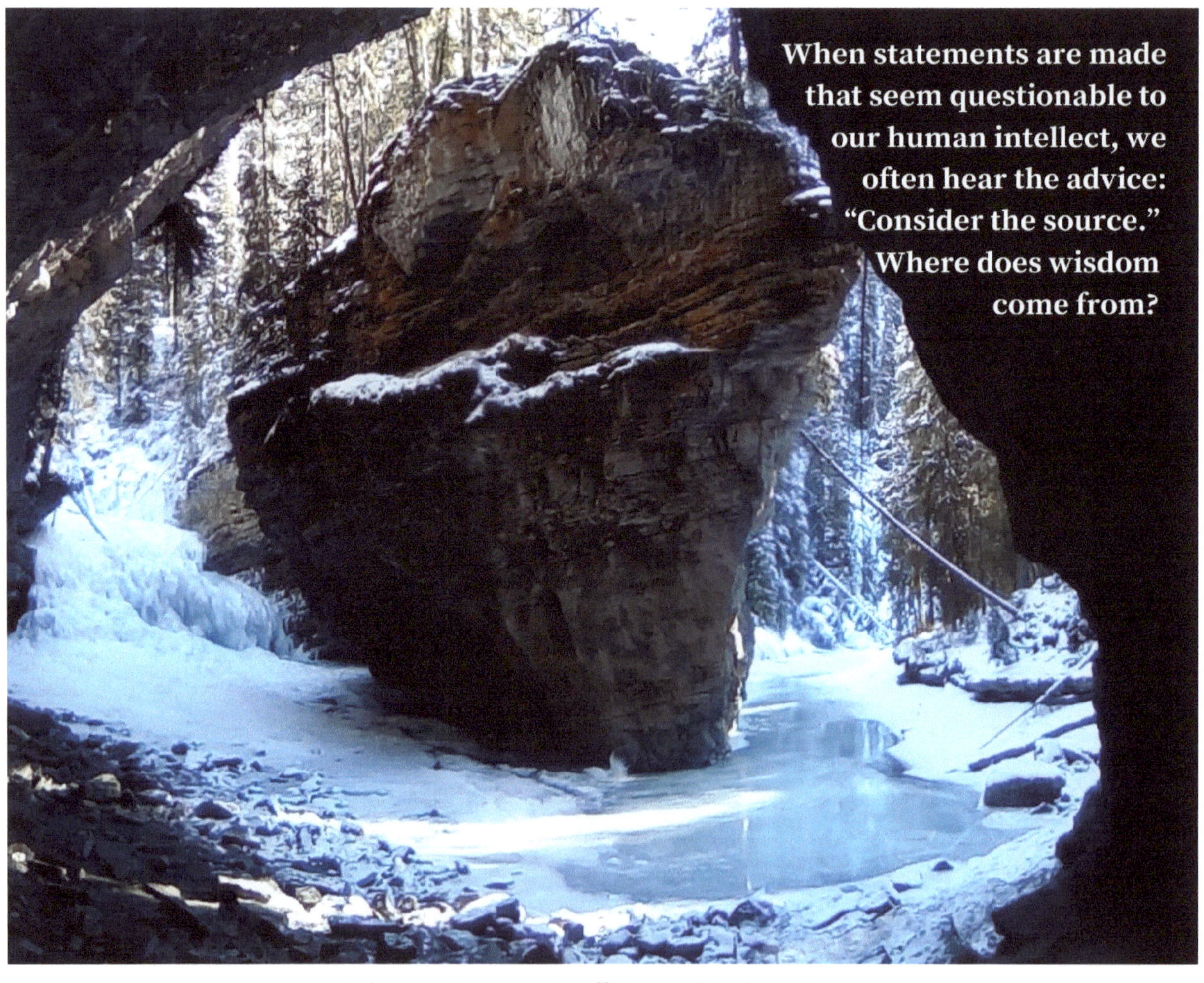

Johnston Canyon – Banff National Park – Alberta

Consider the Source

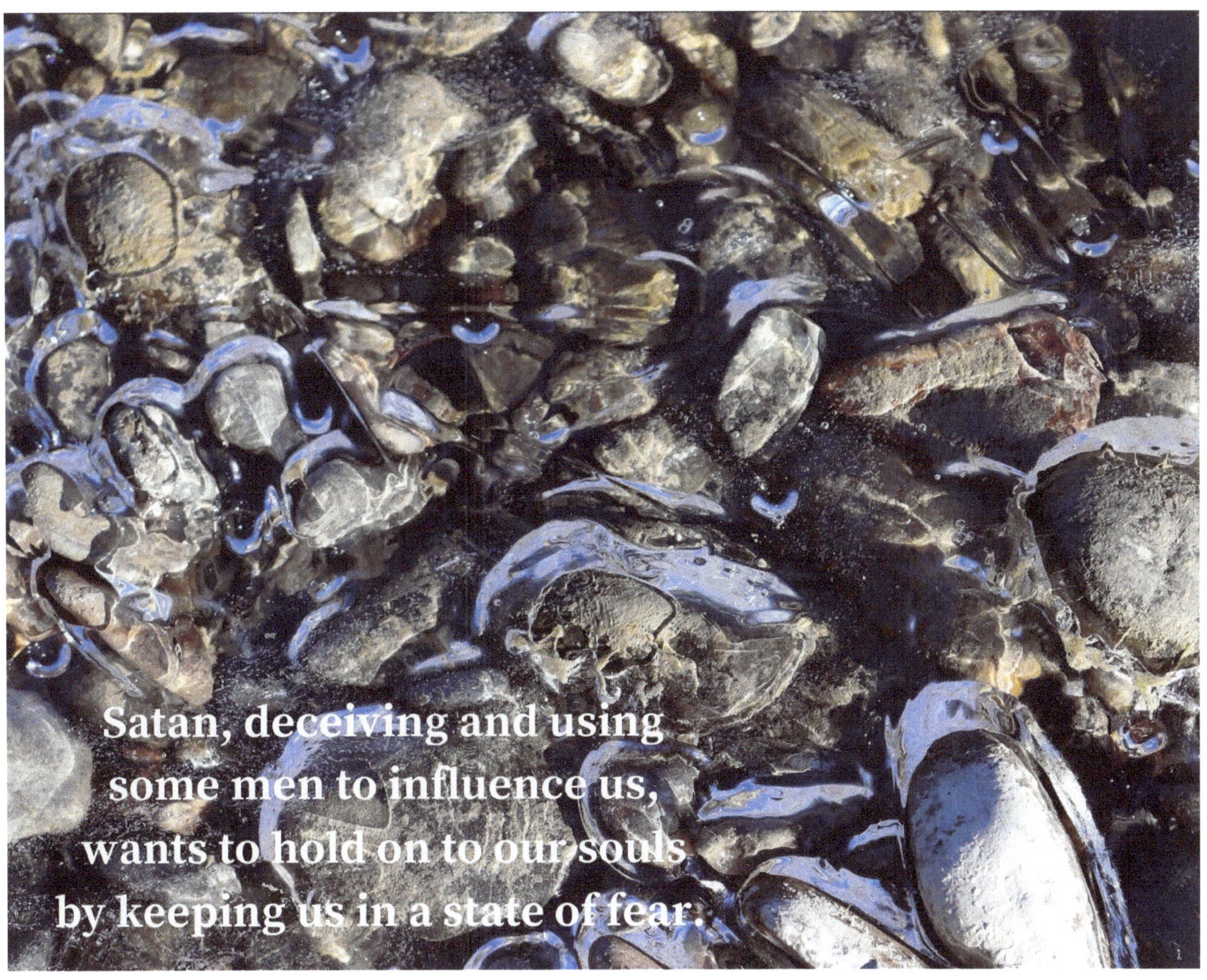

River Rocks with First Ice – Blaeberry River – British Columbia

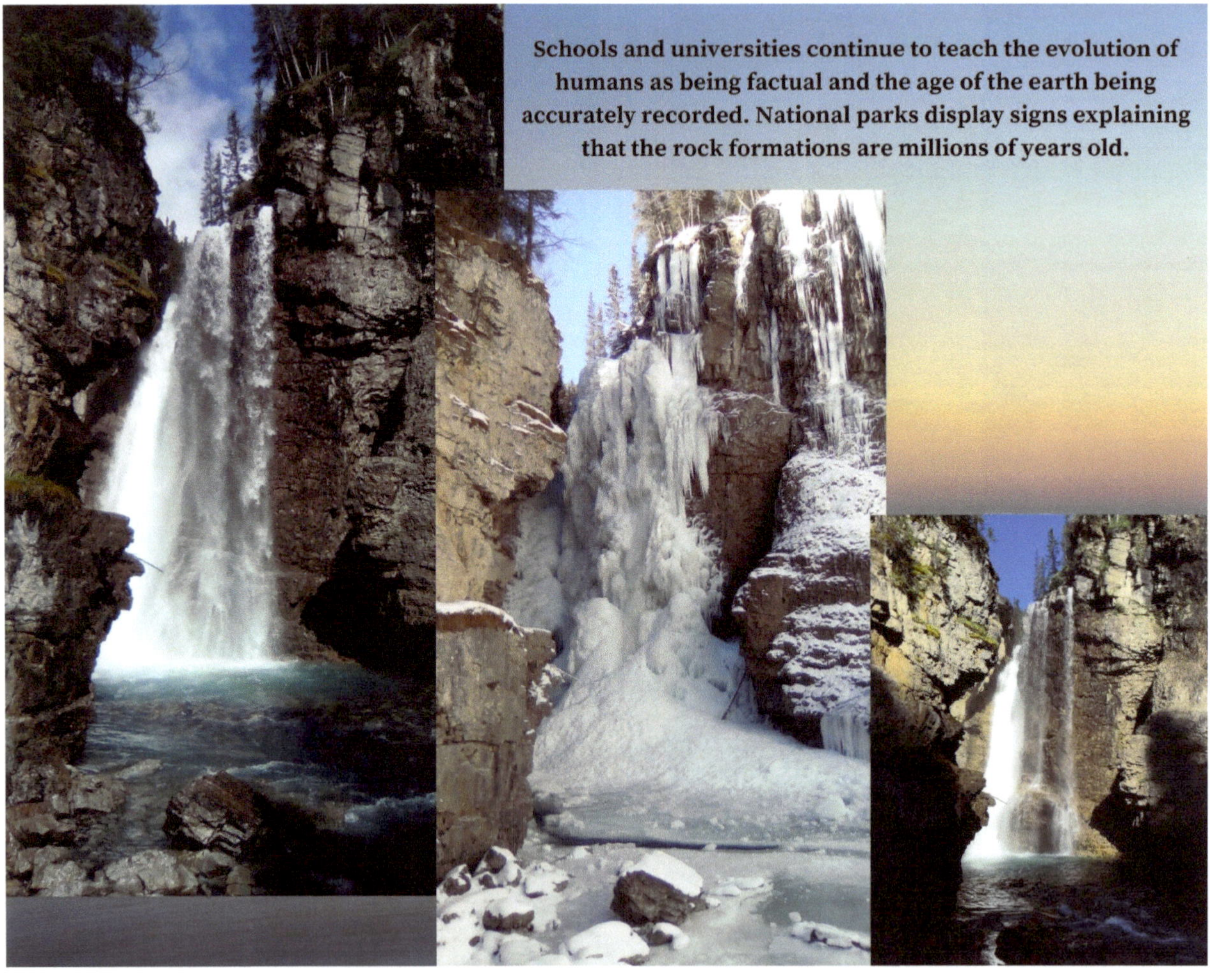

Johnston Canyon Upper Falls – Banff National Park – Alberta

4

Admit and Repent

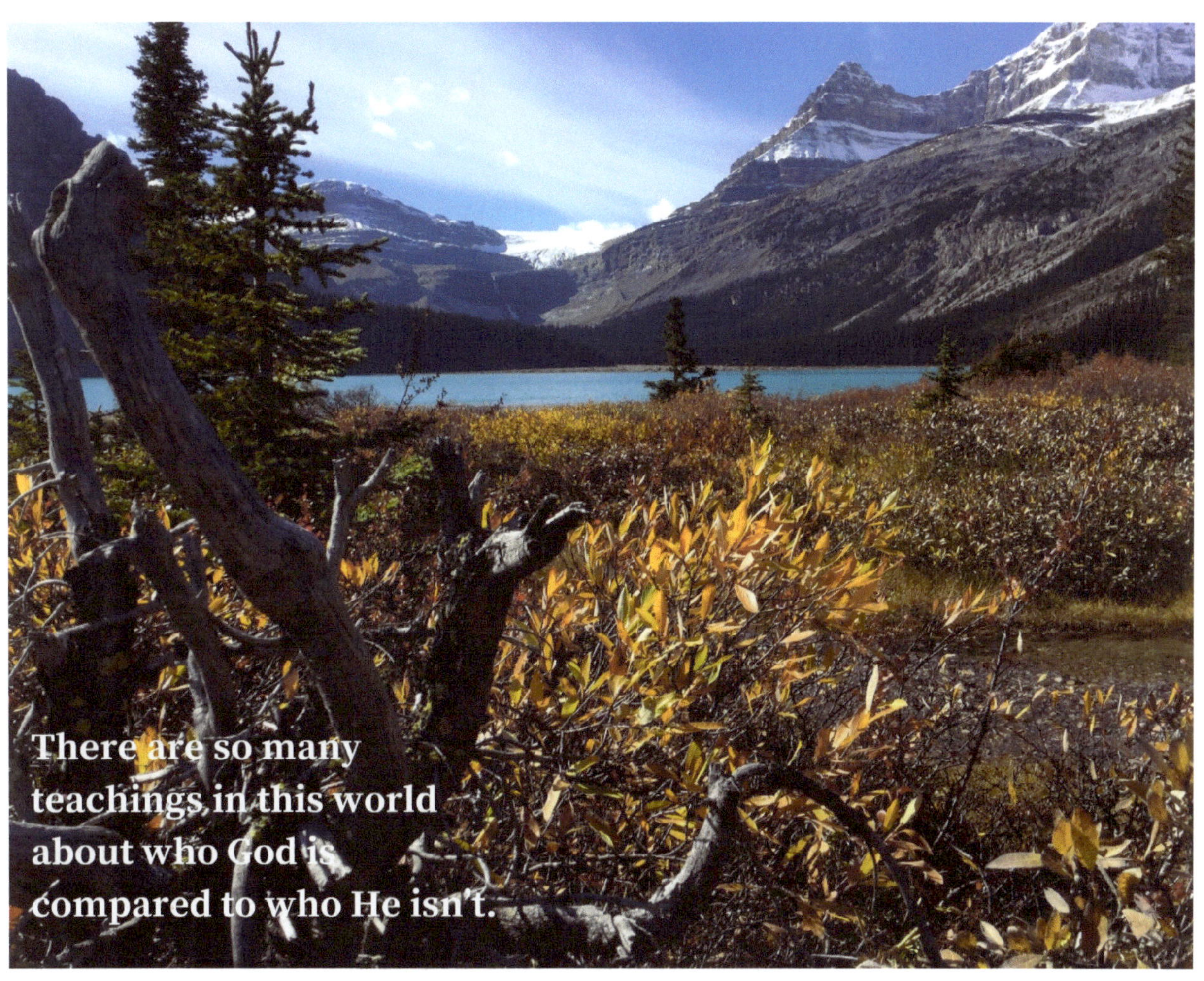

Bow Lake – Banff National Park – Alberta

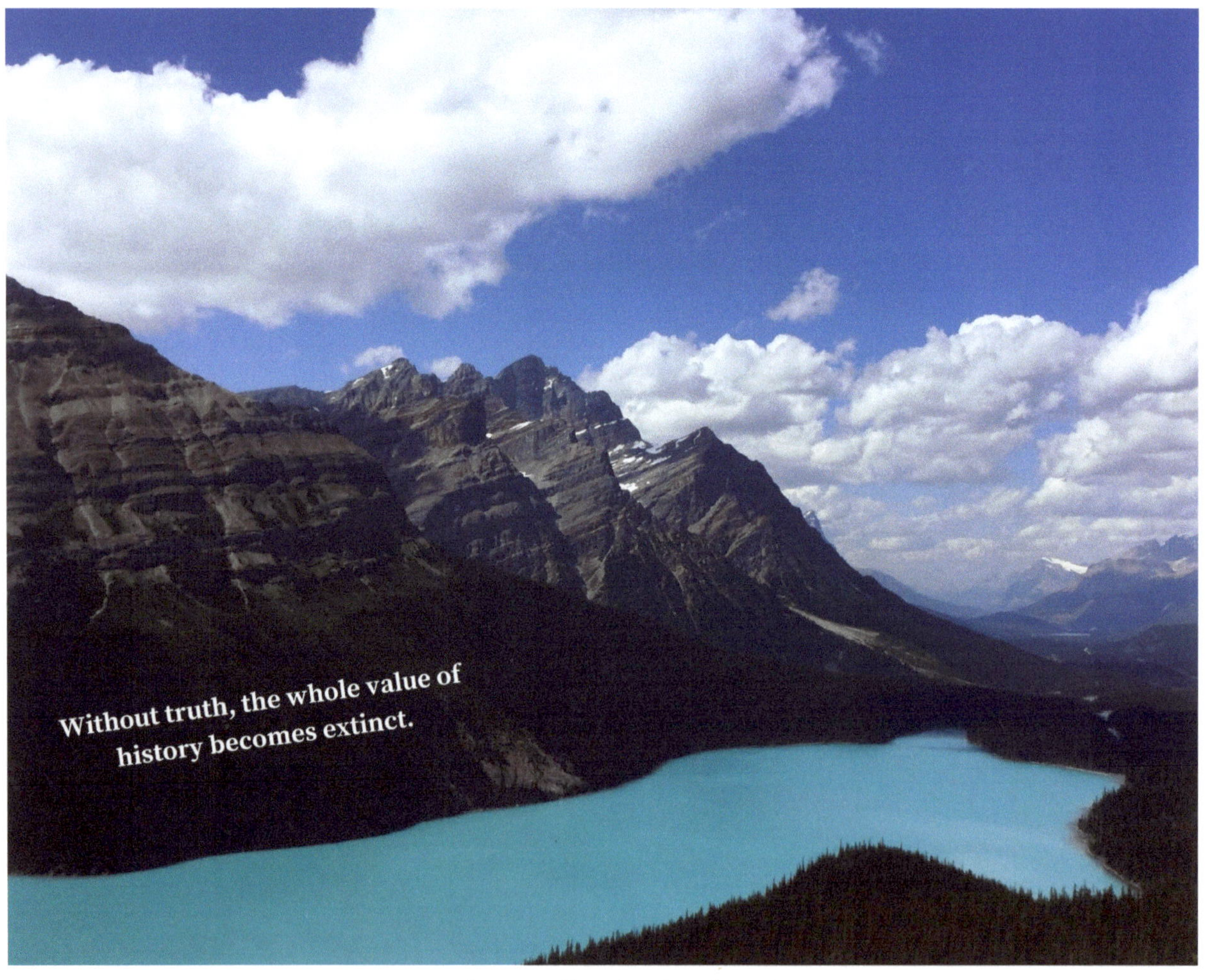

Peyto Lake – Banff National Park – Alberta

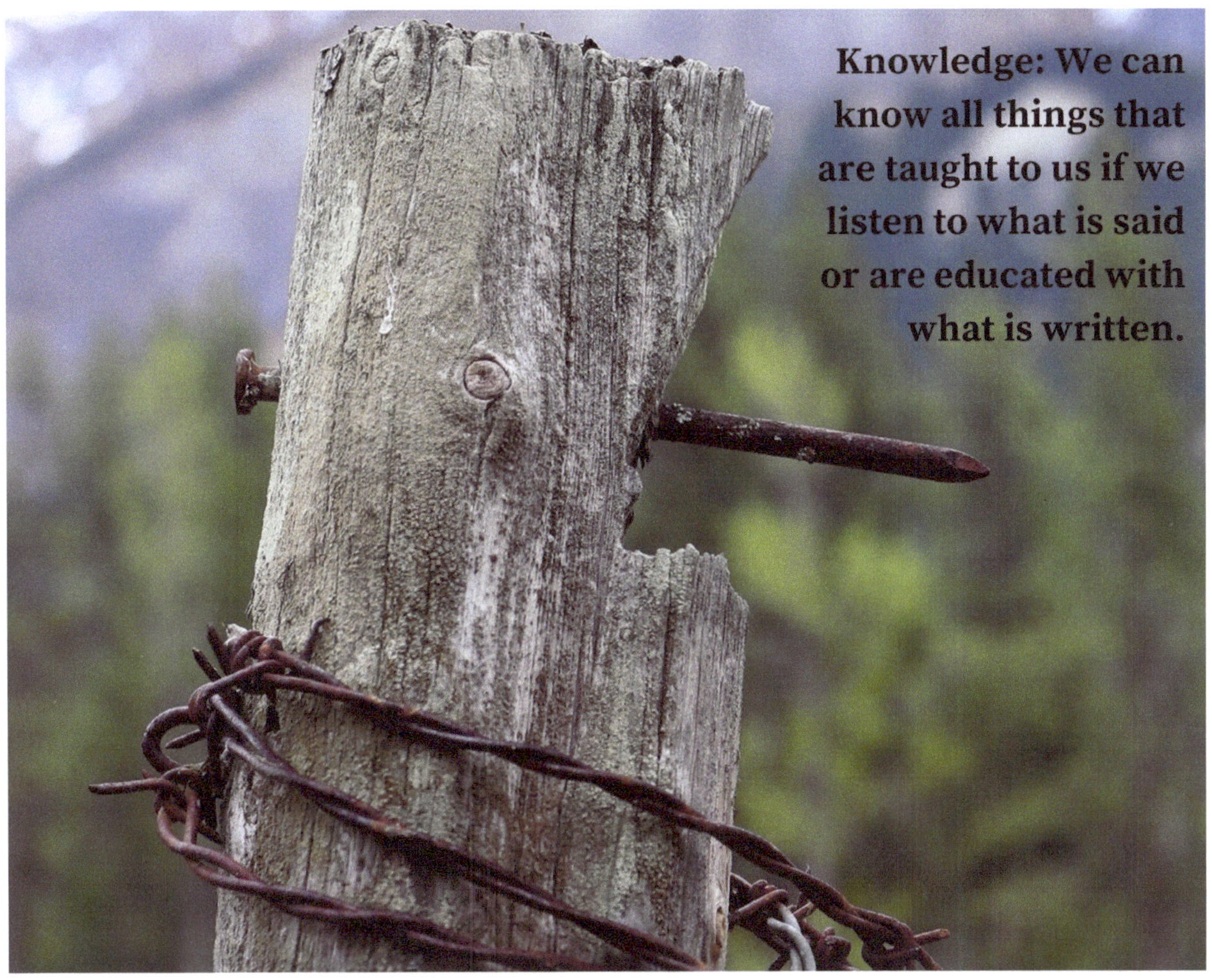

Rusty Old Fence Nail in Focus – Blaeberry Valley – British Columbia

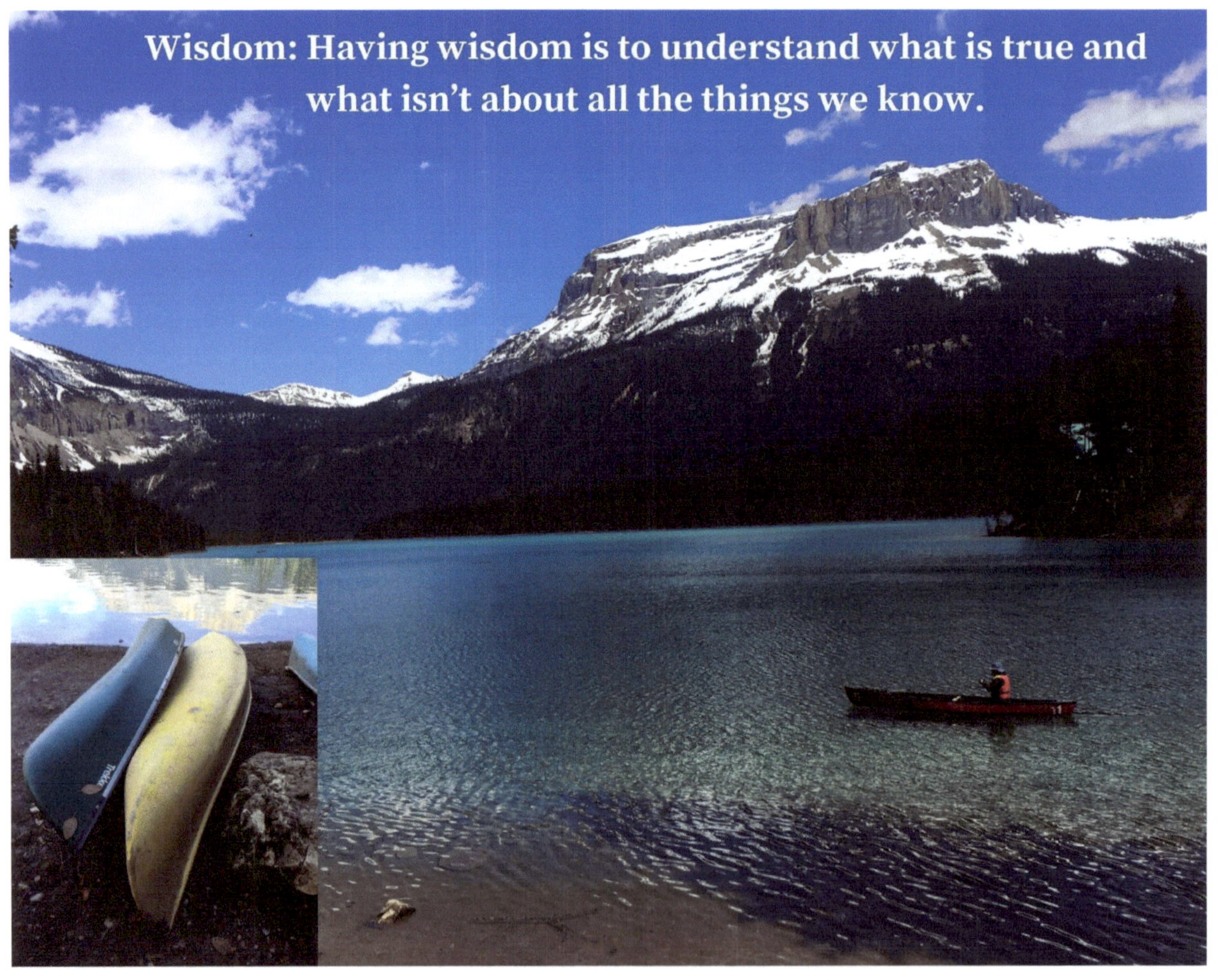

Emerald Lake – Yoho National Park – British Columbia

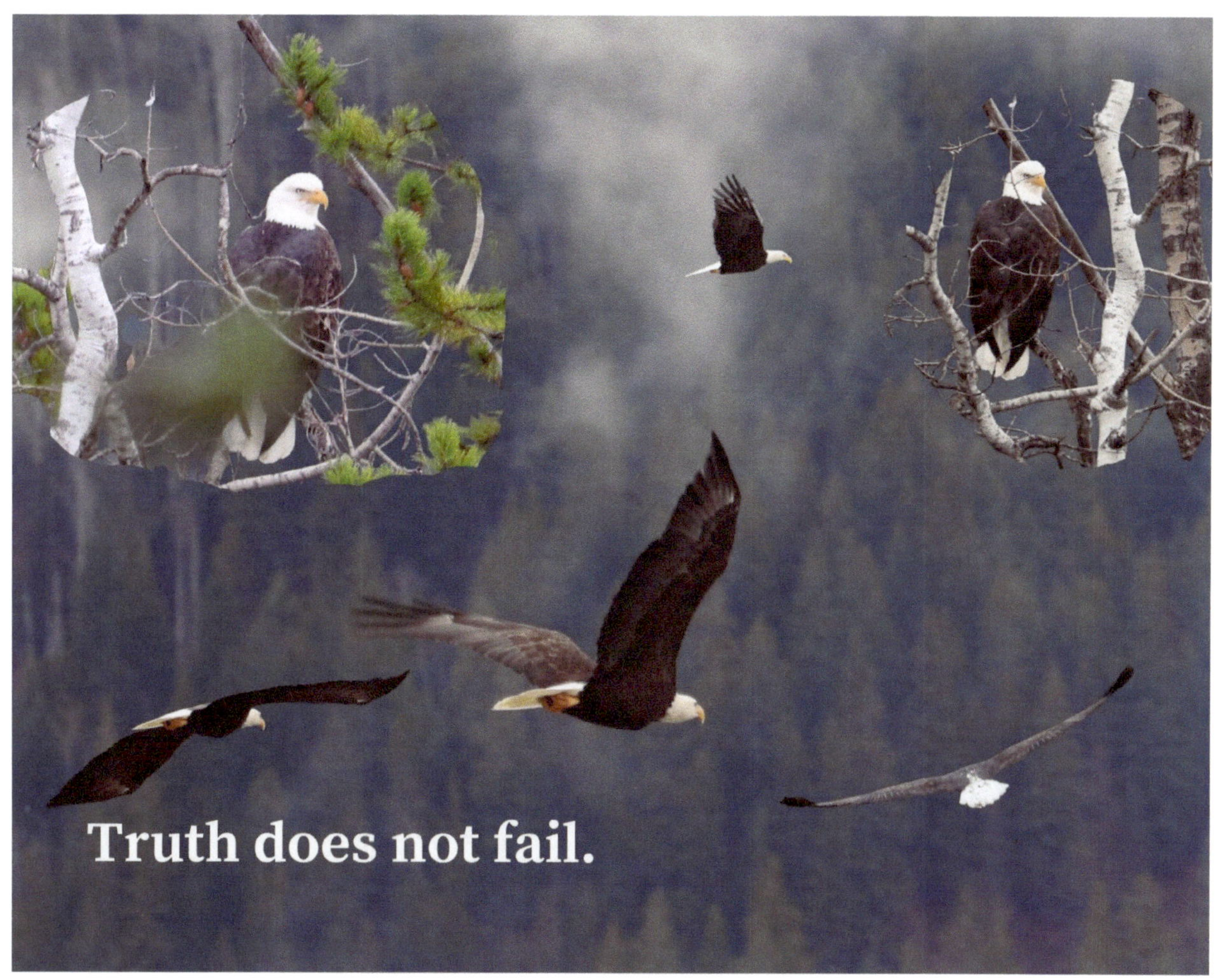

Bald Eagles – Blaeberry Valley – British Columbia

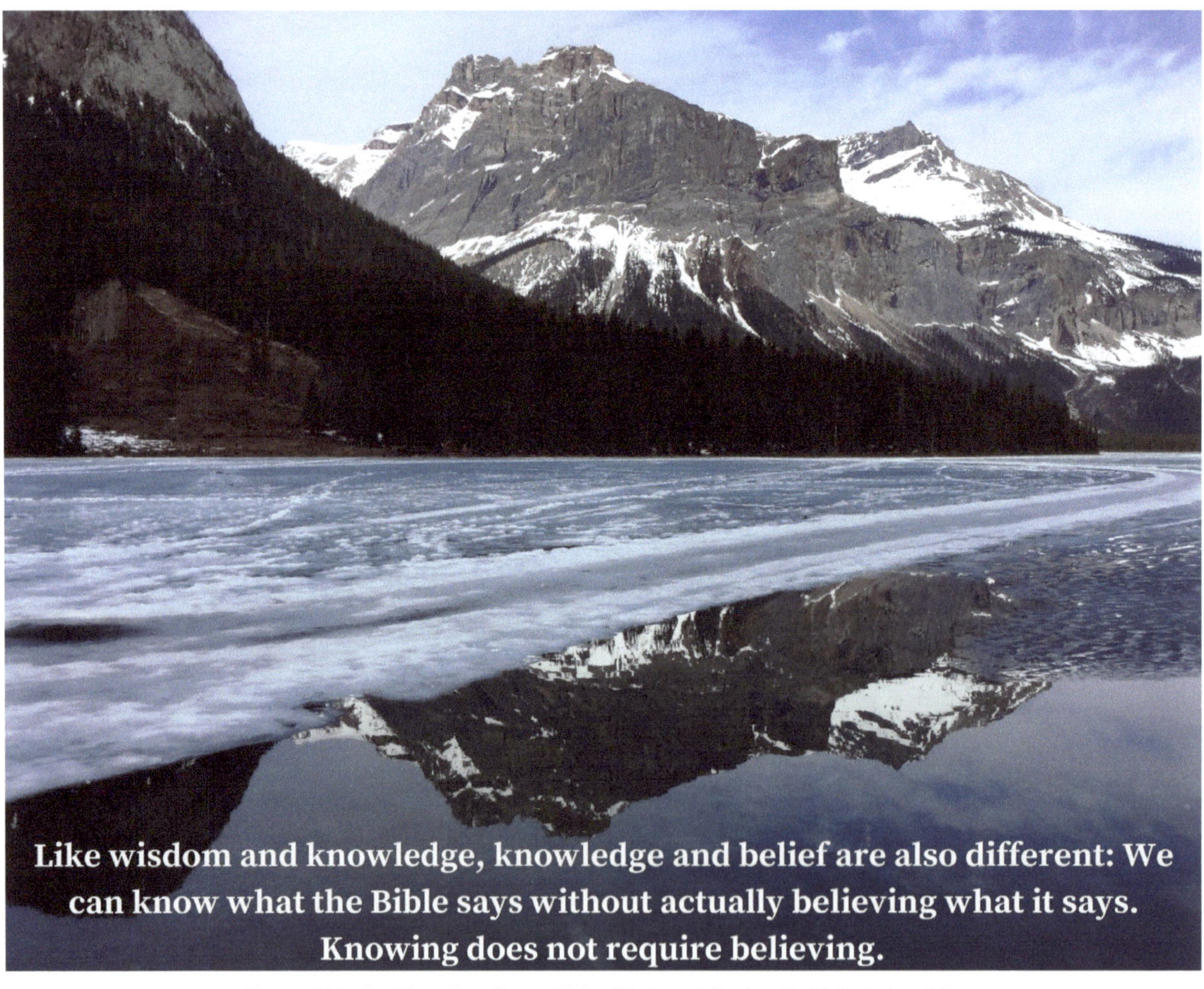

Emerald Lake Thawing Out – Yoho National Park – British Columbia

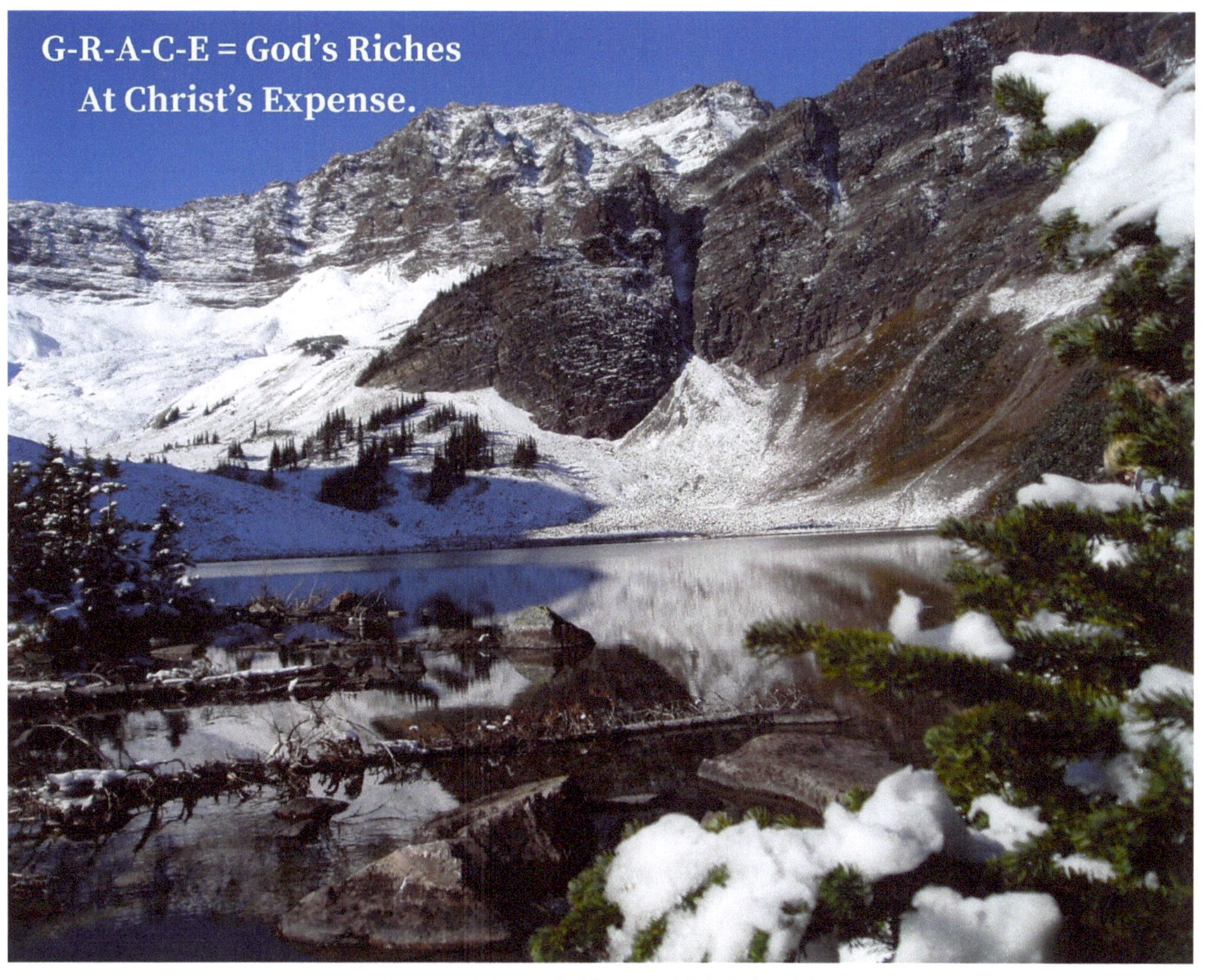

Gorman Lake – Golden – British Columbia

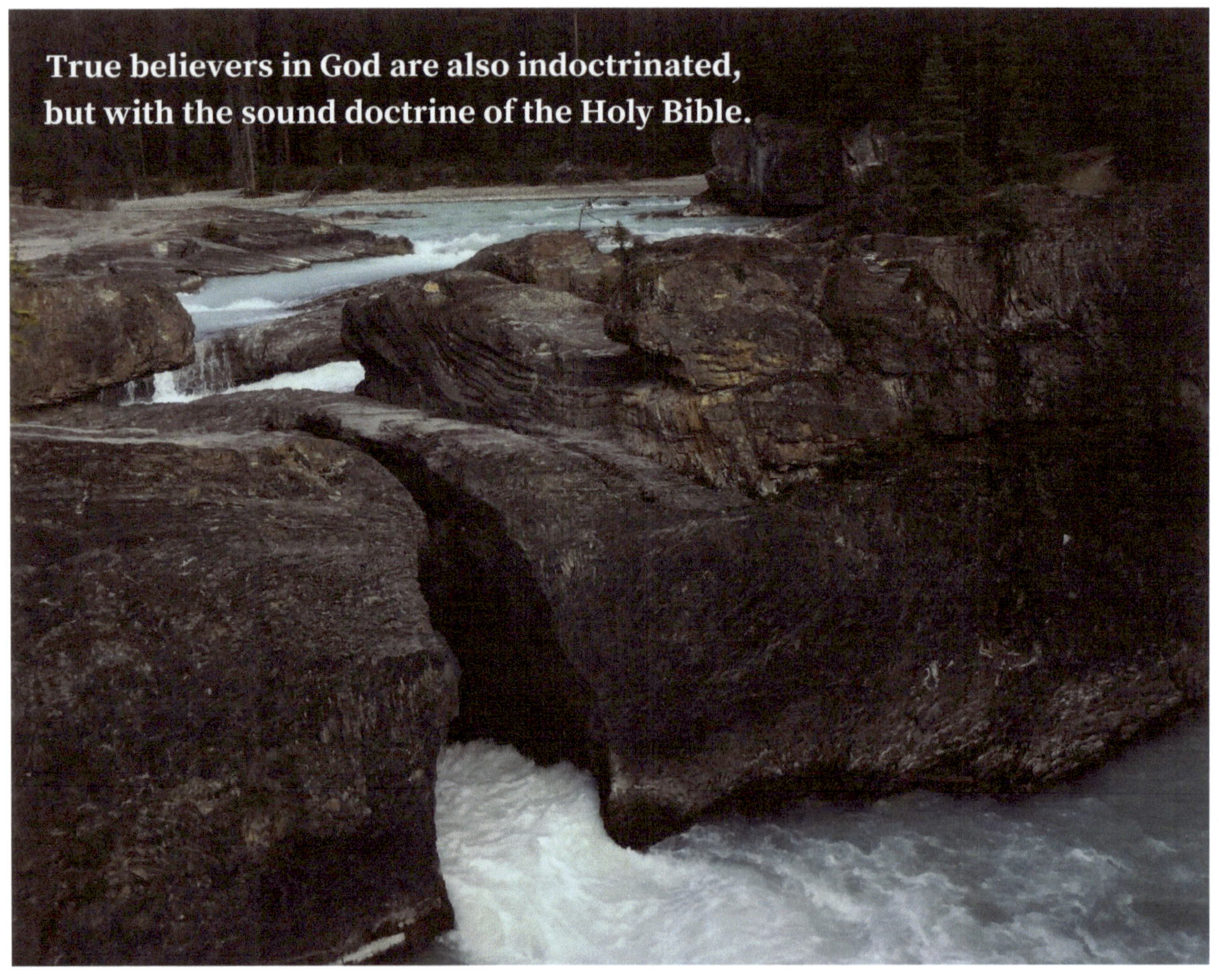

Natural Bridge – Yoho National Park – British Columbia

5

In Pursuit of Wisdom

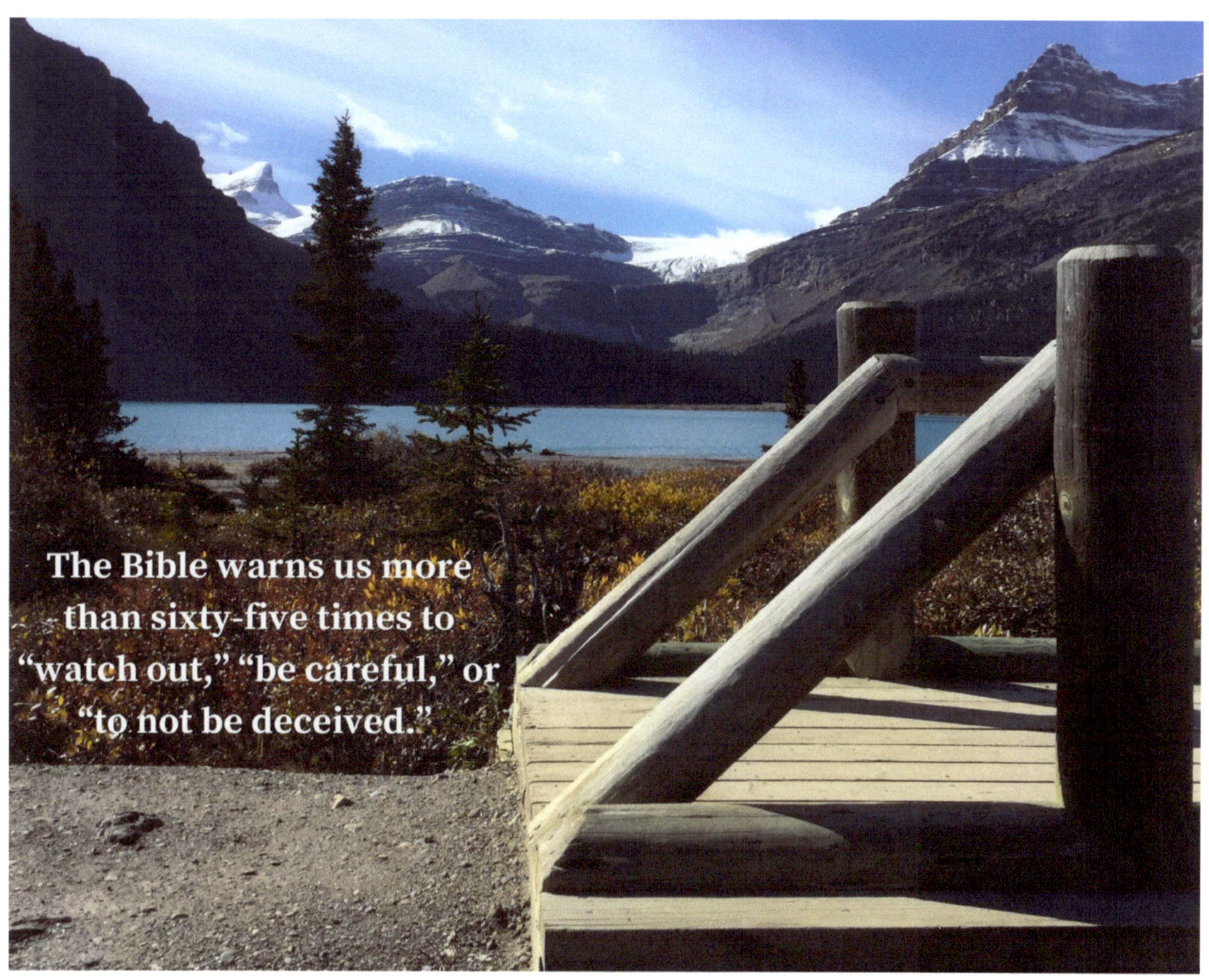

Bow Lake Trail – Banff National Park – Alberta

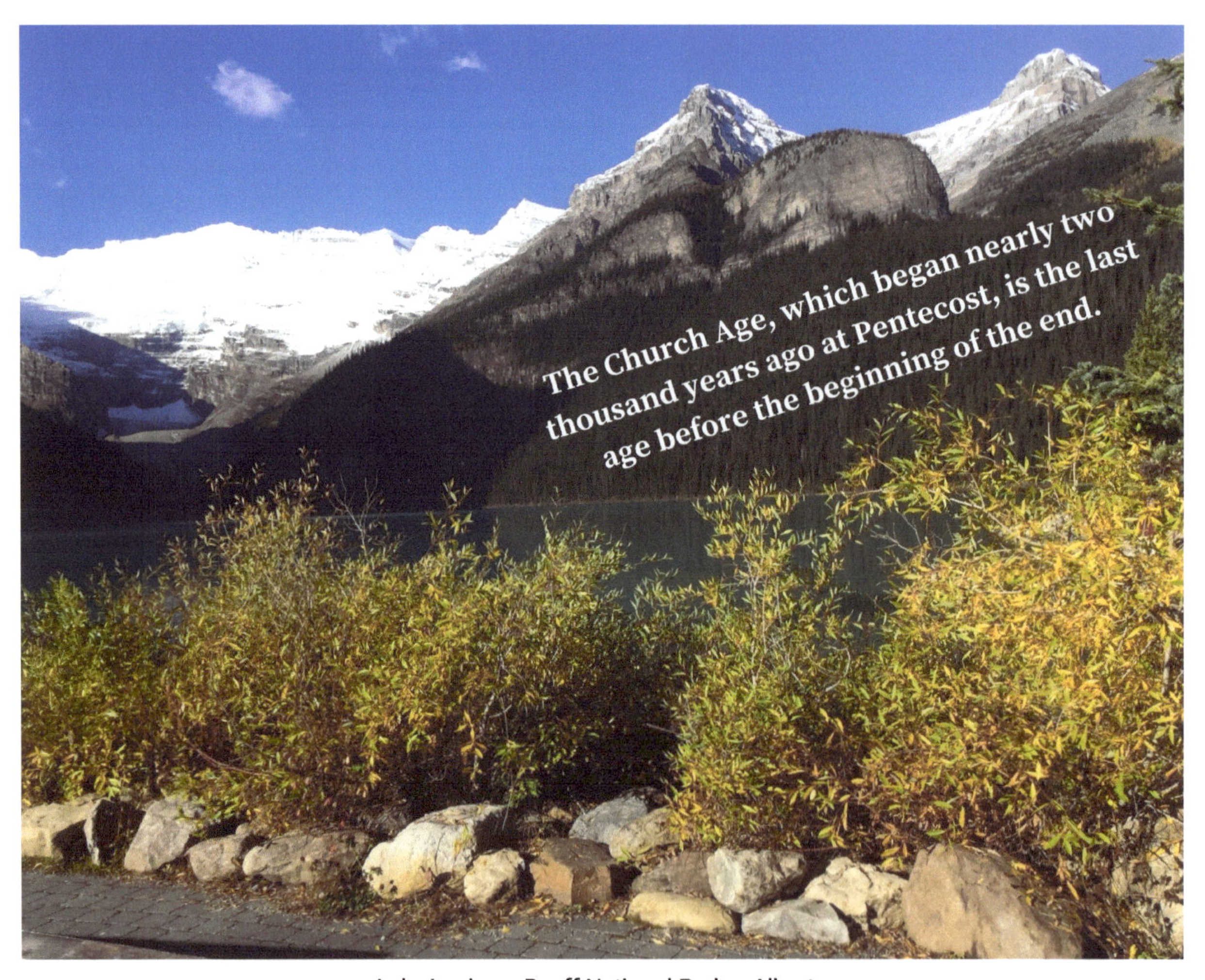

Lake Louise – Banff National Park – Alberta

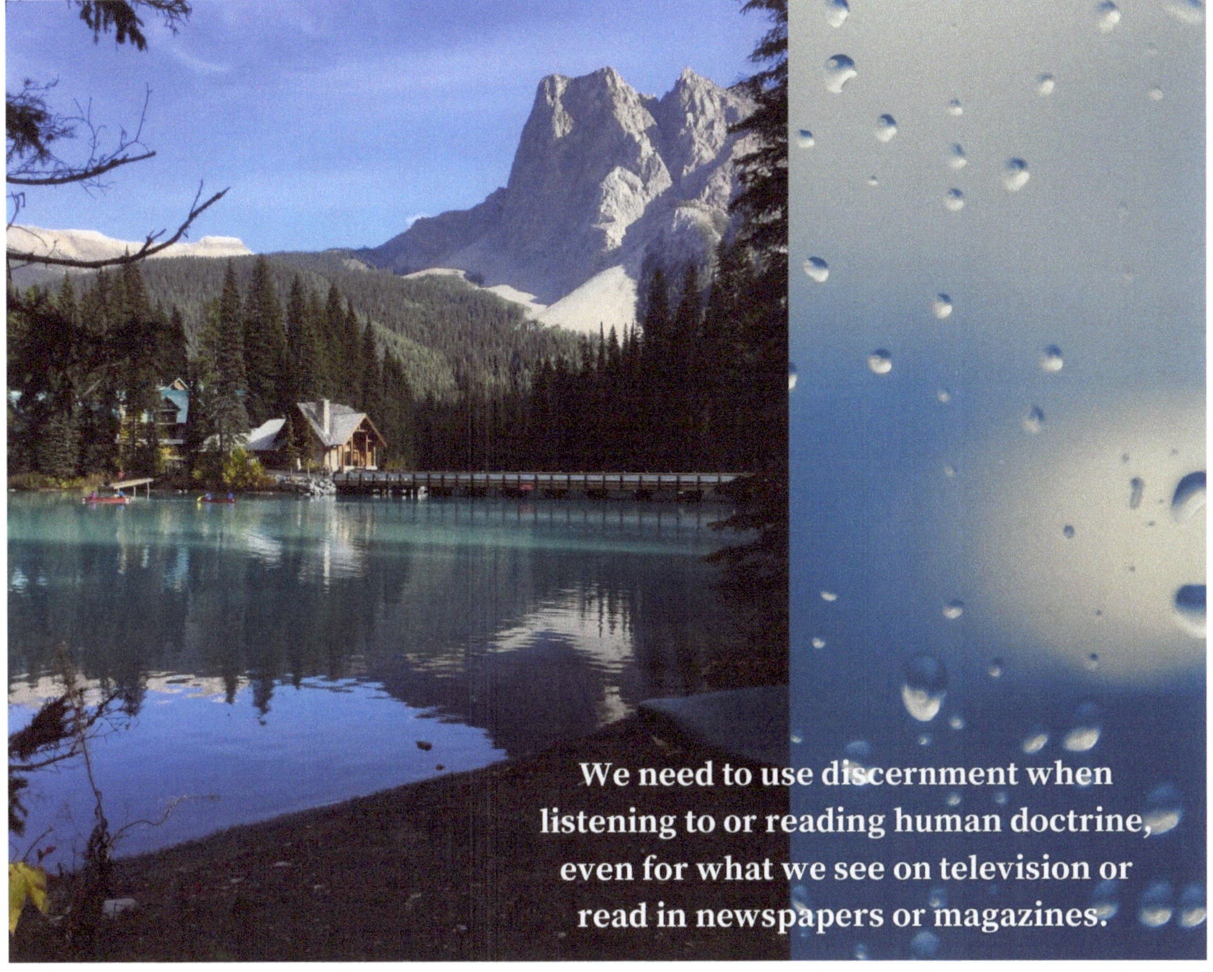

Emerald Lake – Yoho National Park – British Columbia

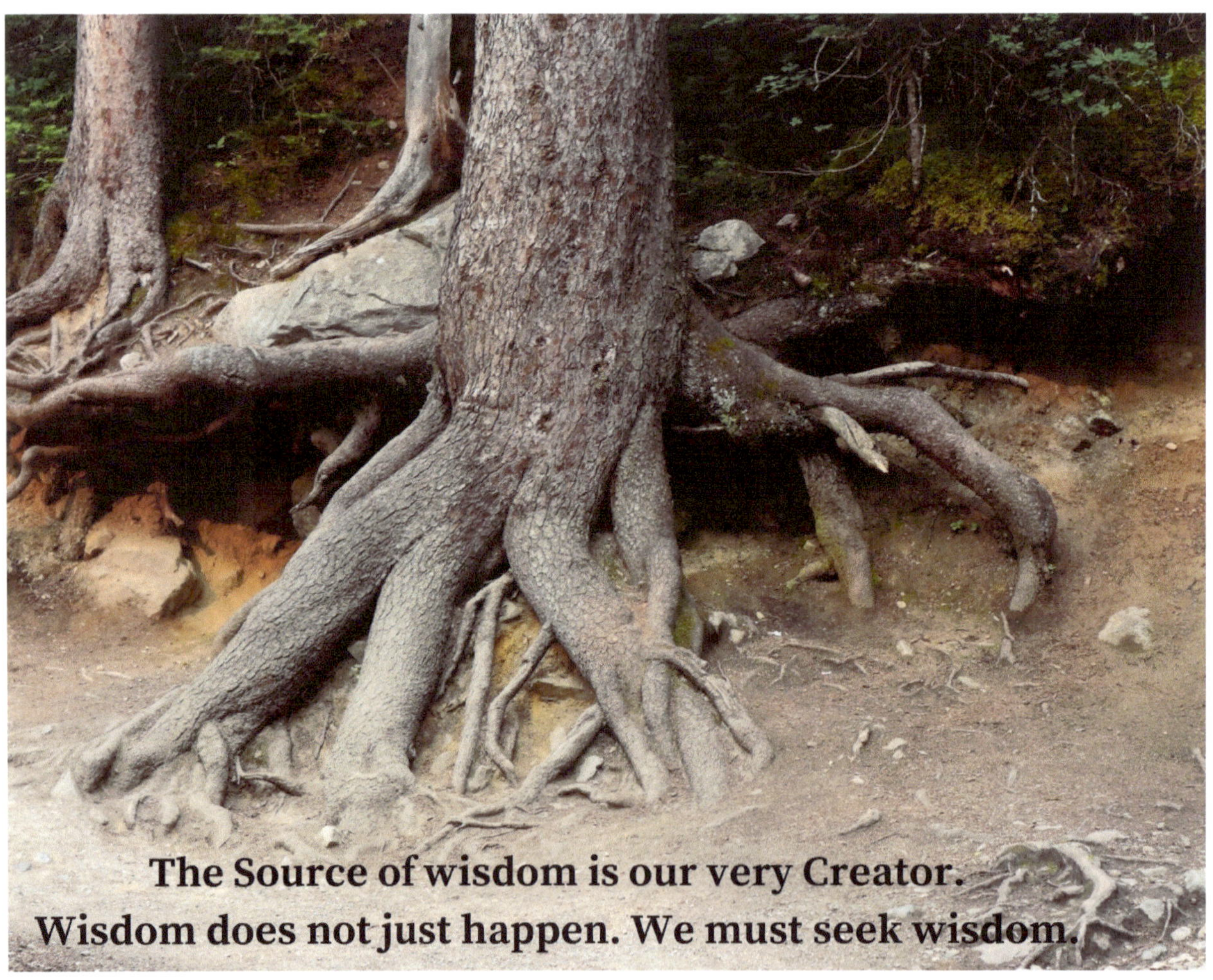

Strong Roots – Lake Agnes Trail – Banff National Park – Alberta

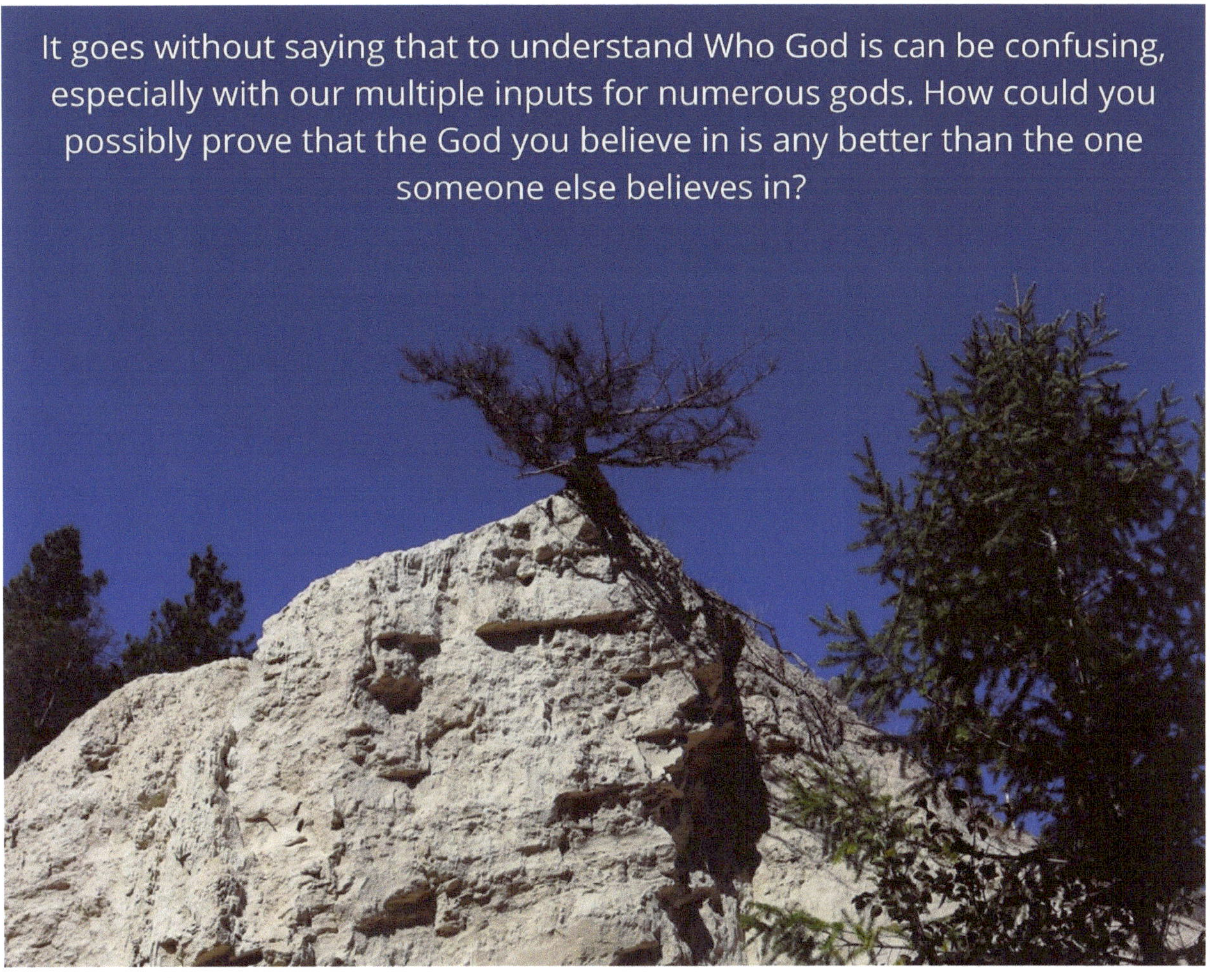

Hoodoos – Fairmont Hot Springs – Columbia Valley – British Columbia

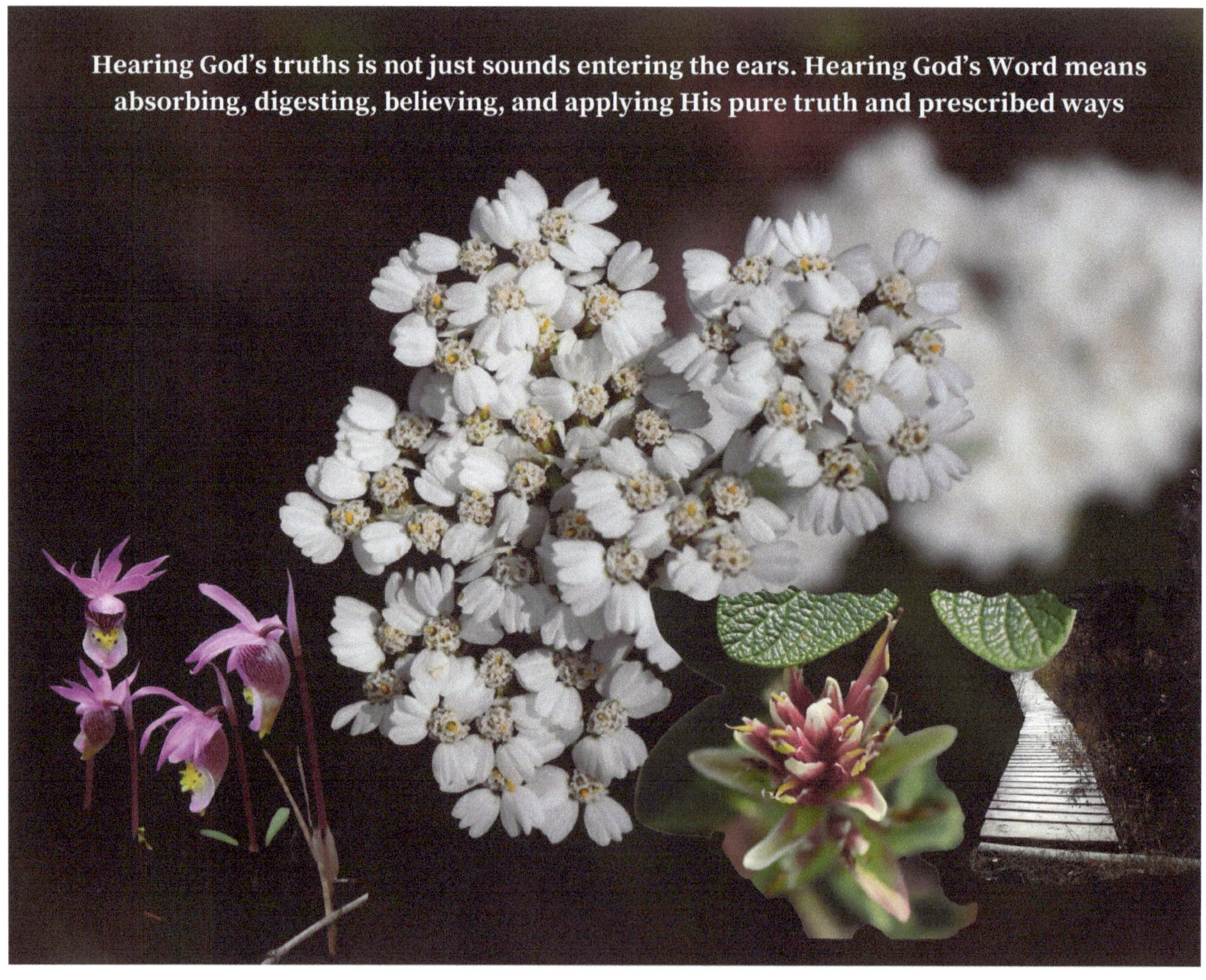

Rocky Mountain Flowers – Canadian Rocky Mountains – British Columbia / Alberta

6

Wisdom Found by Listening

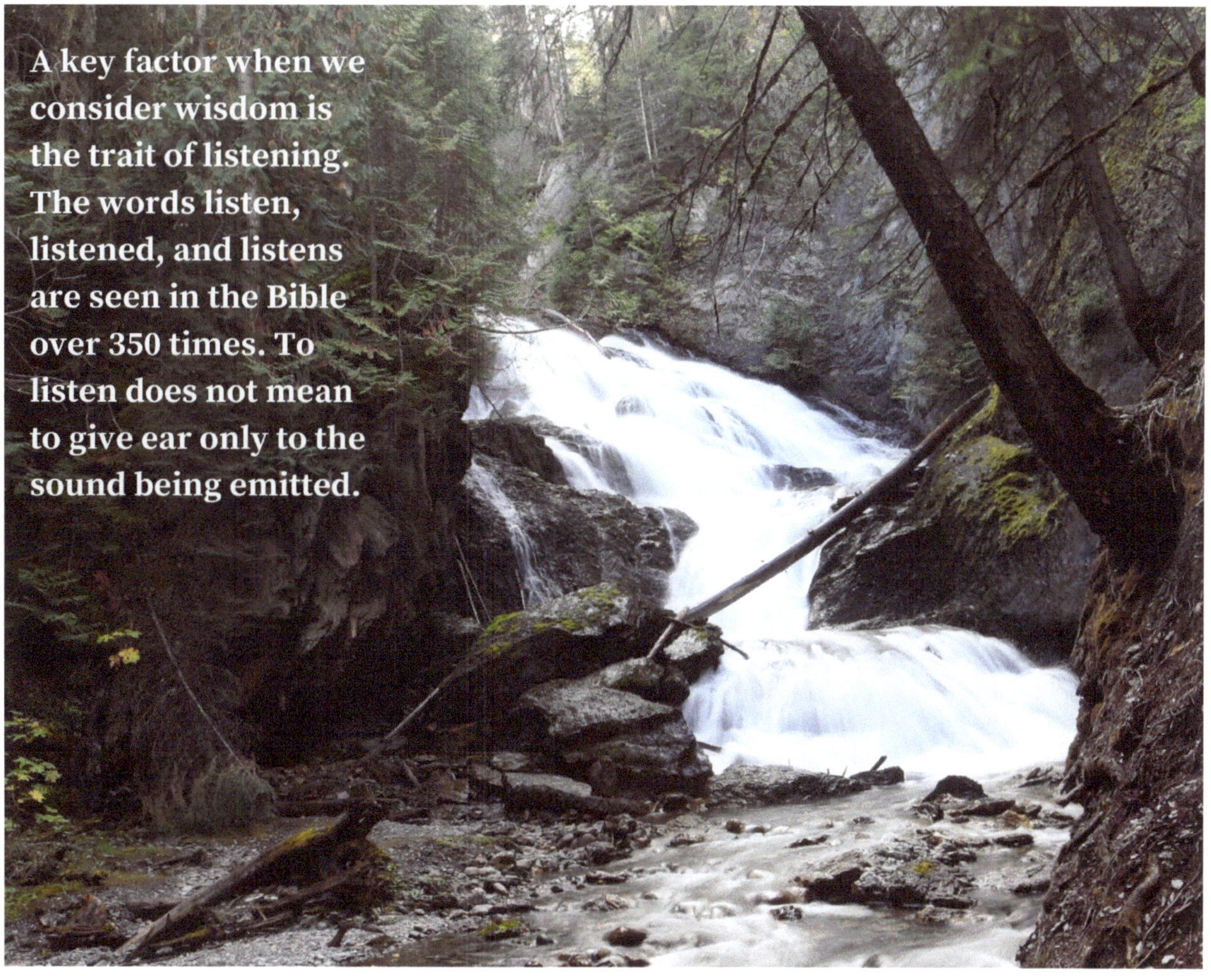

Salmon Stream – Columbia Valley – British Columbia

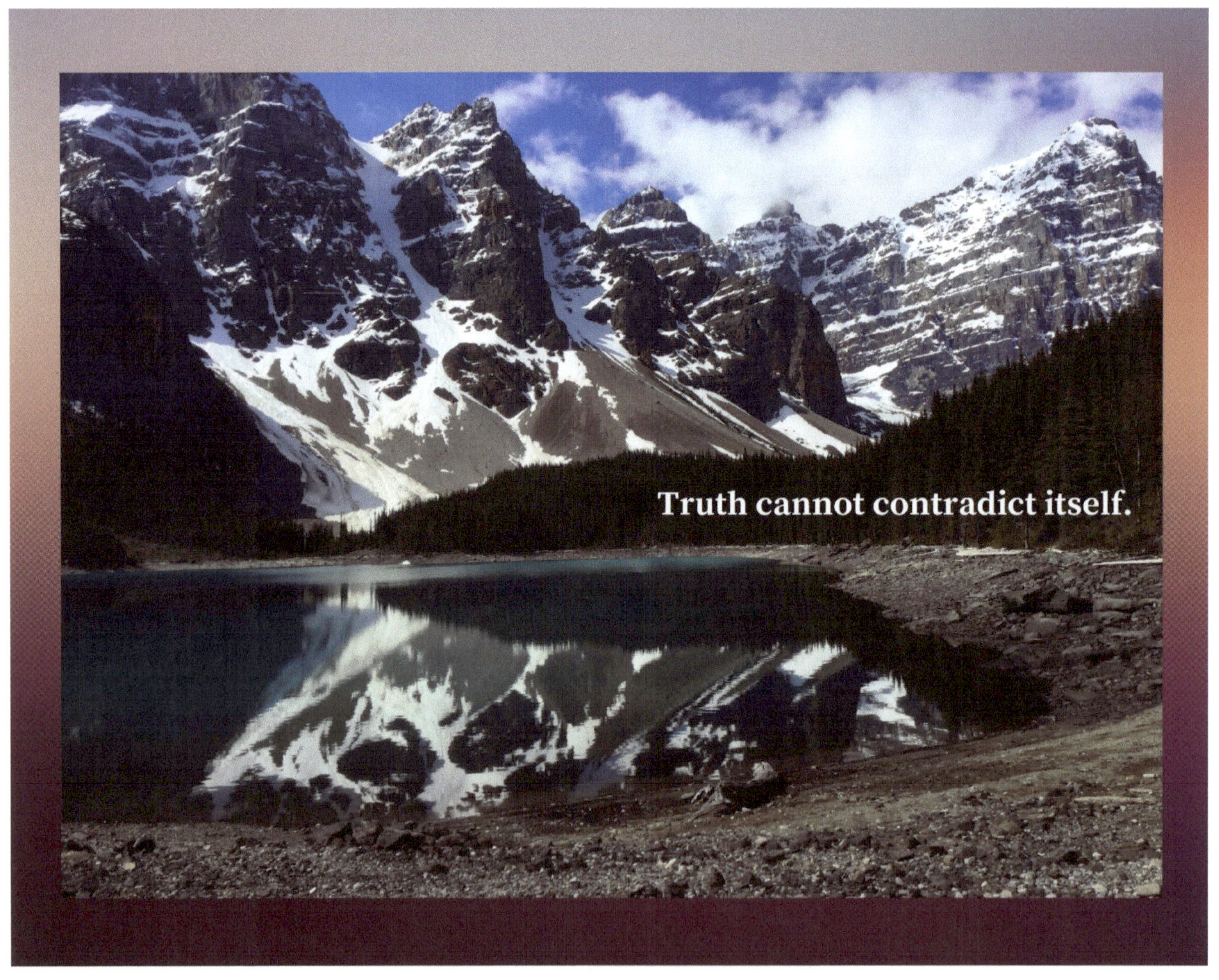

Moraine Lake – Banff National Park – Alberta

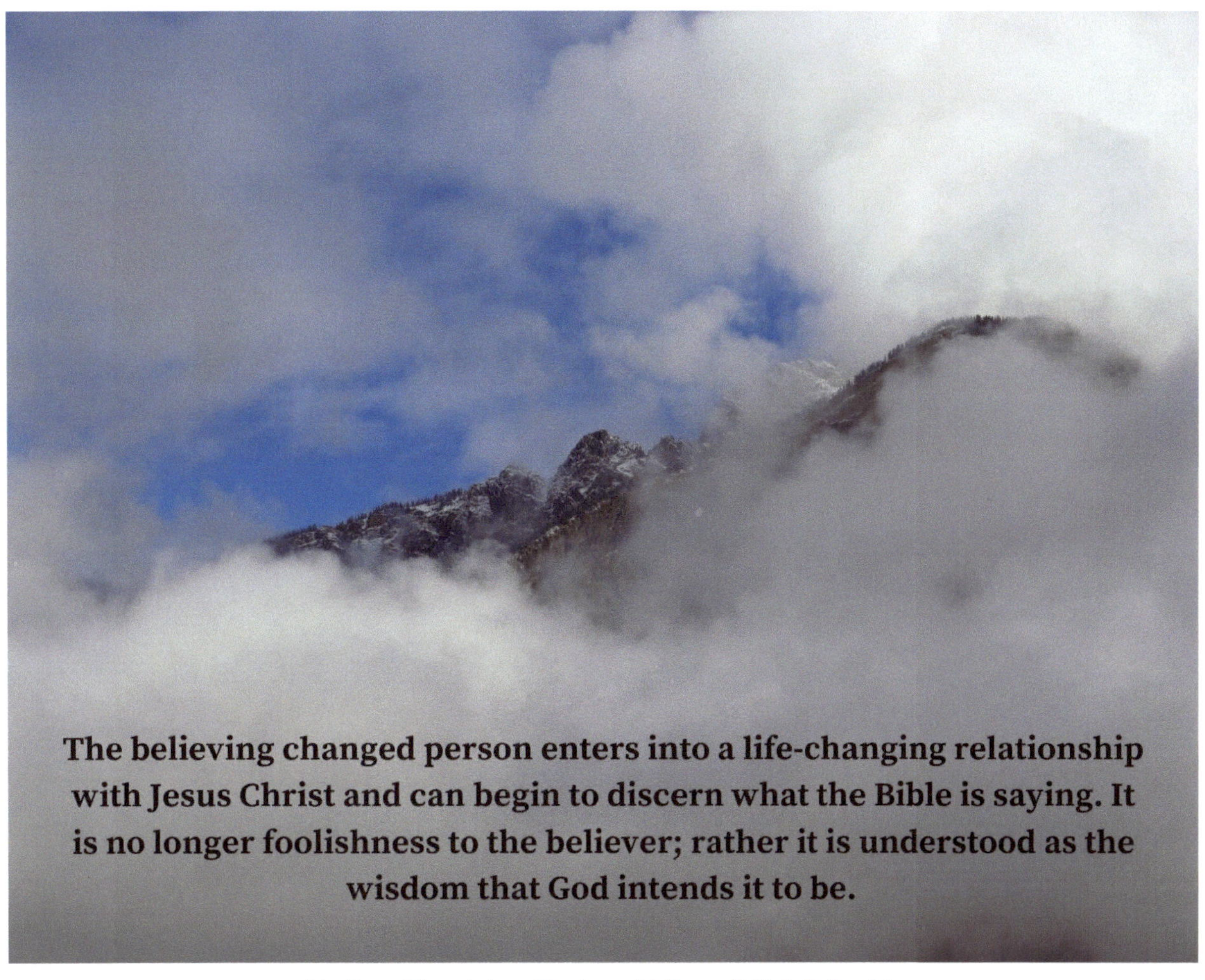

Hedberg Mountain – Blaeberry Valley – British Columbia

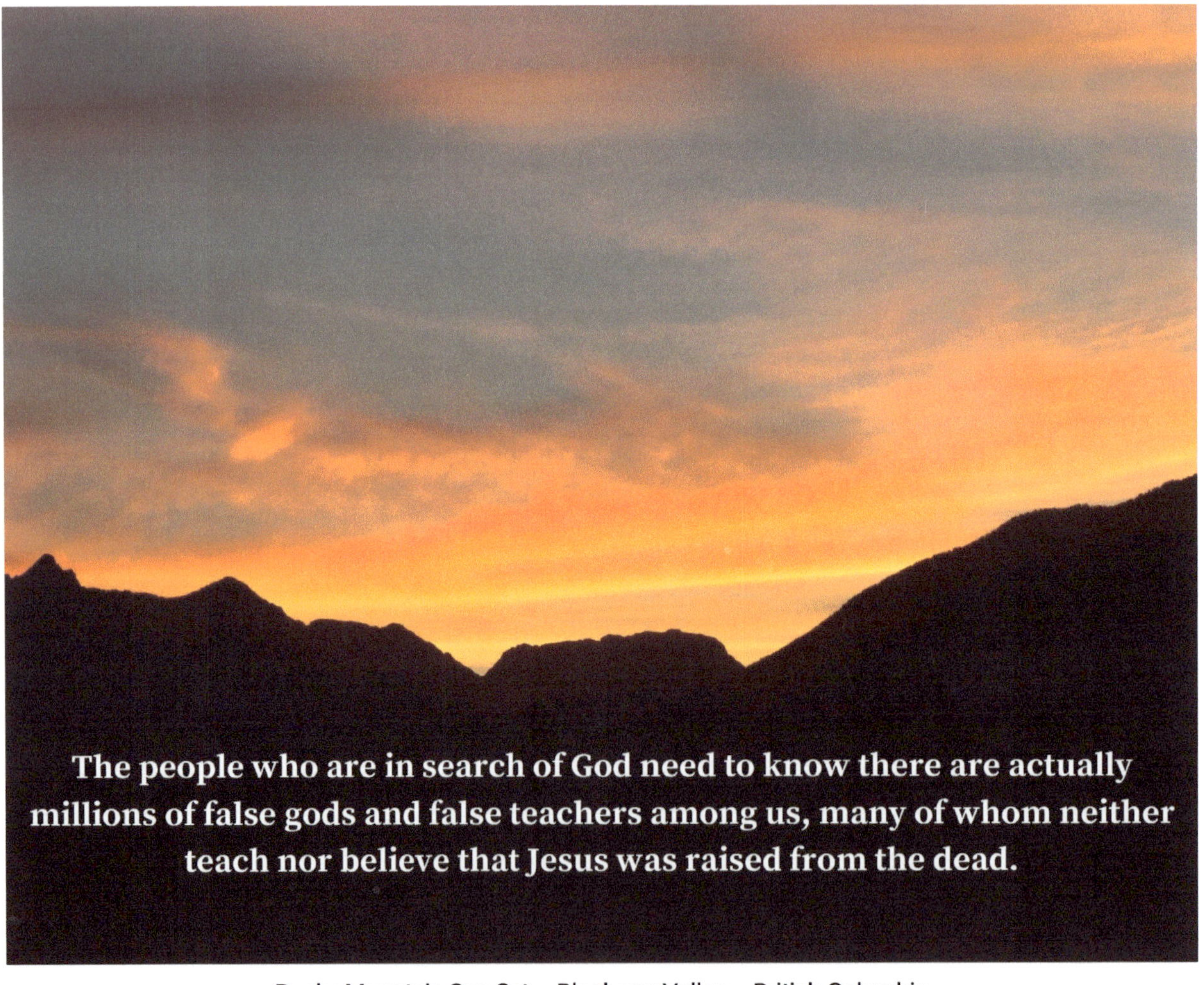

Rocky Mountain Sun Set – Blaeberry Valley – British Columbia

The most horrible
thing about taking
the mark is that
there is no more
opportunity,
no more hope.

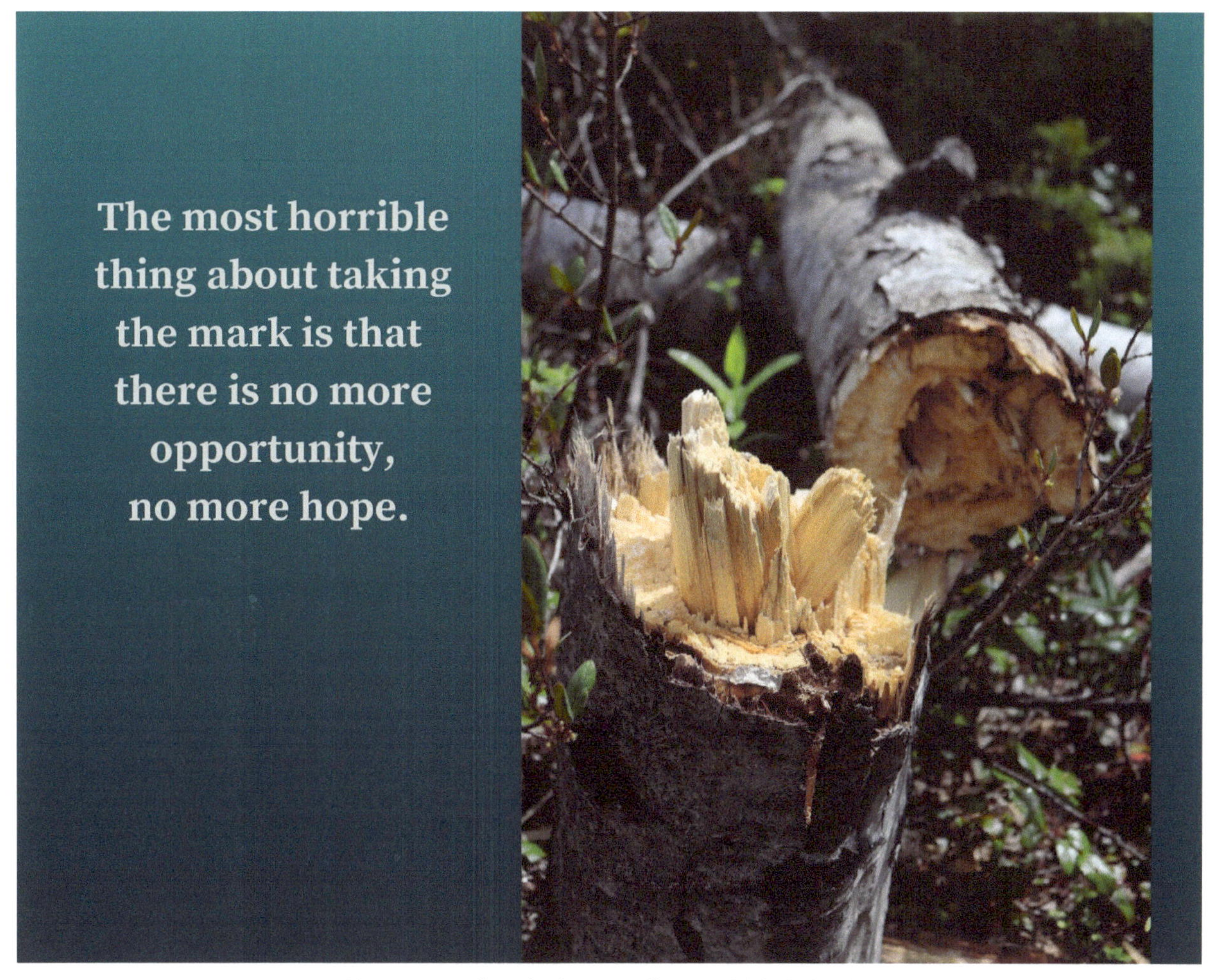

Disconnected – Blaeberry Valley – British Columbia

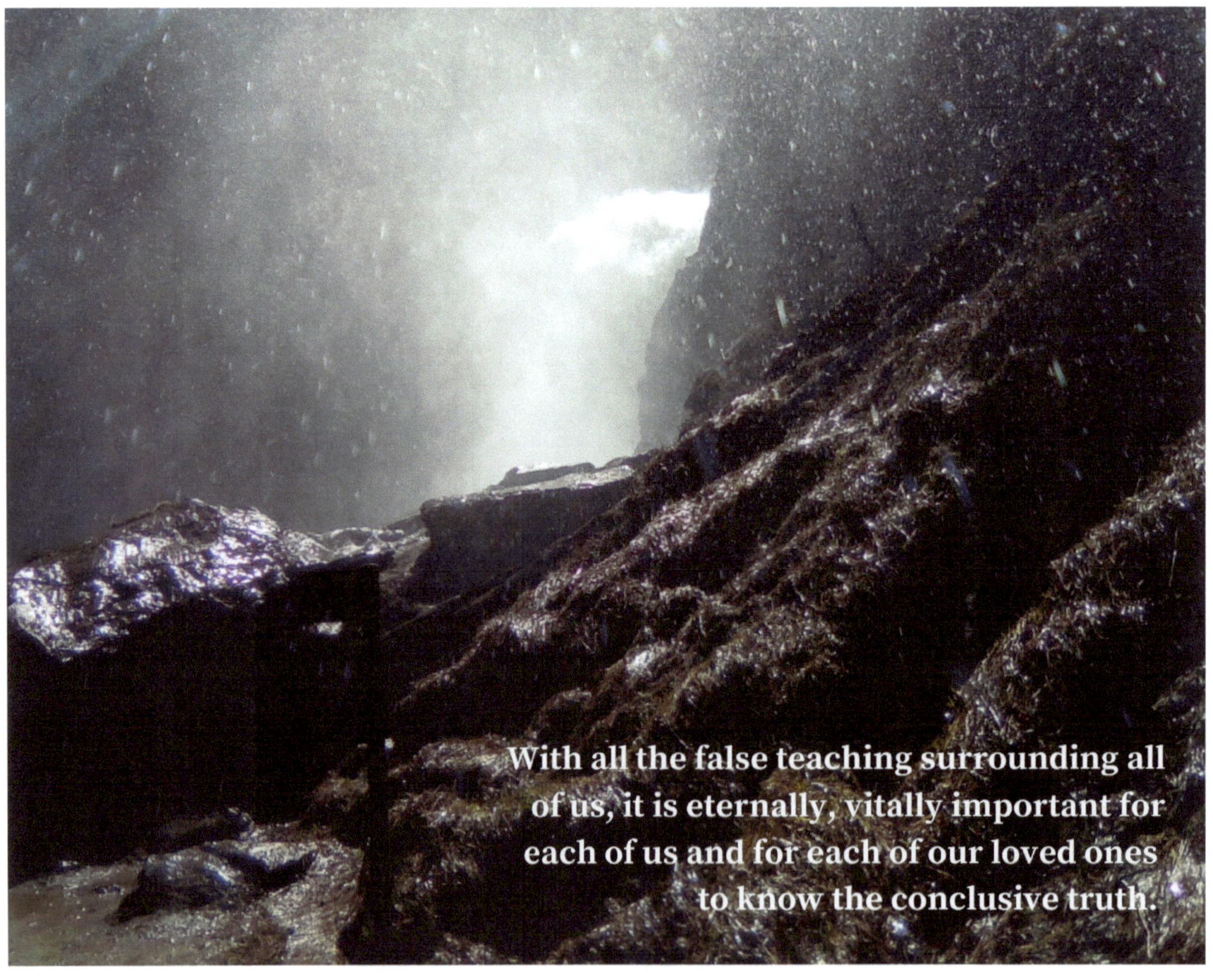

Bear Falls – Glacier National Park – British Columbia

Wisdom in Voting

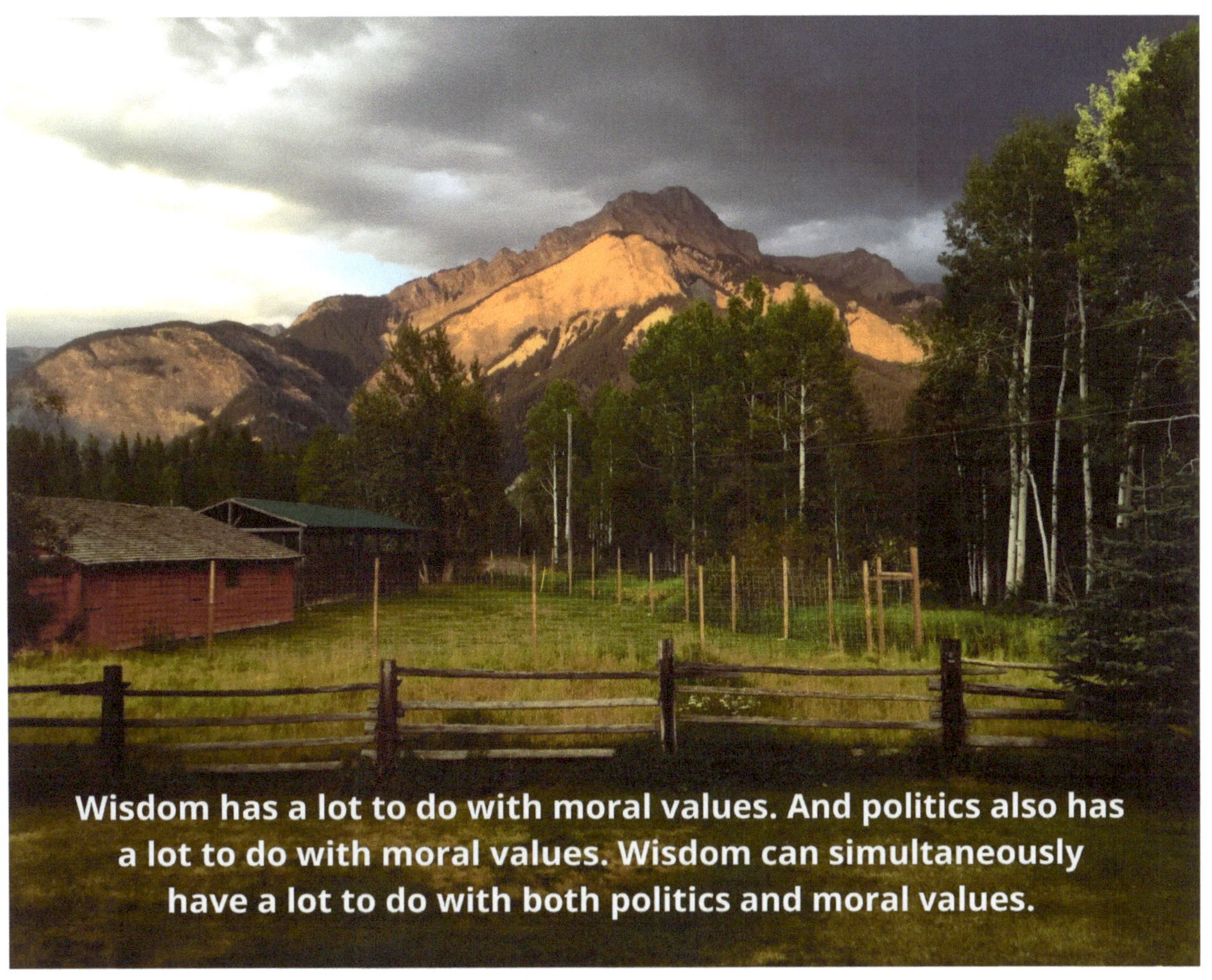

Sunset on Hedberg – Blaeberry Valley – British Columbia

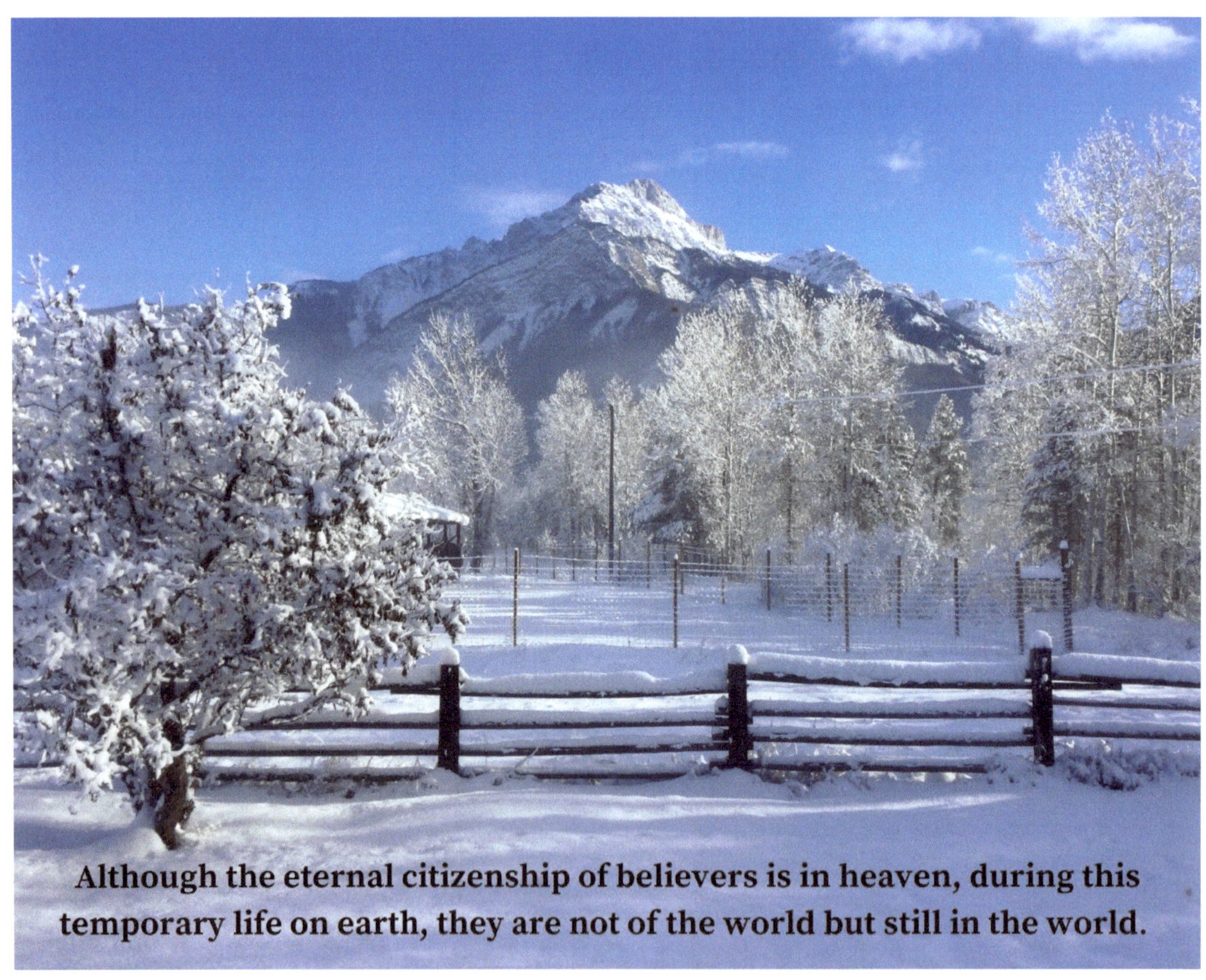

Winter Wonderland – Blaeberry Valley – British Columbia

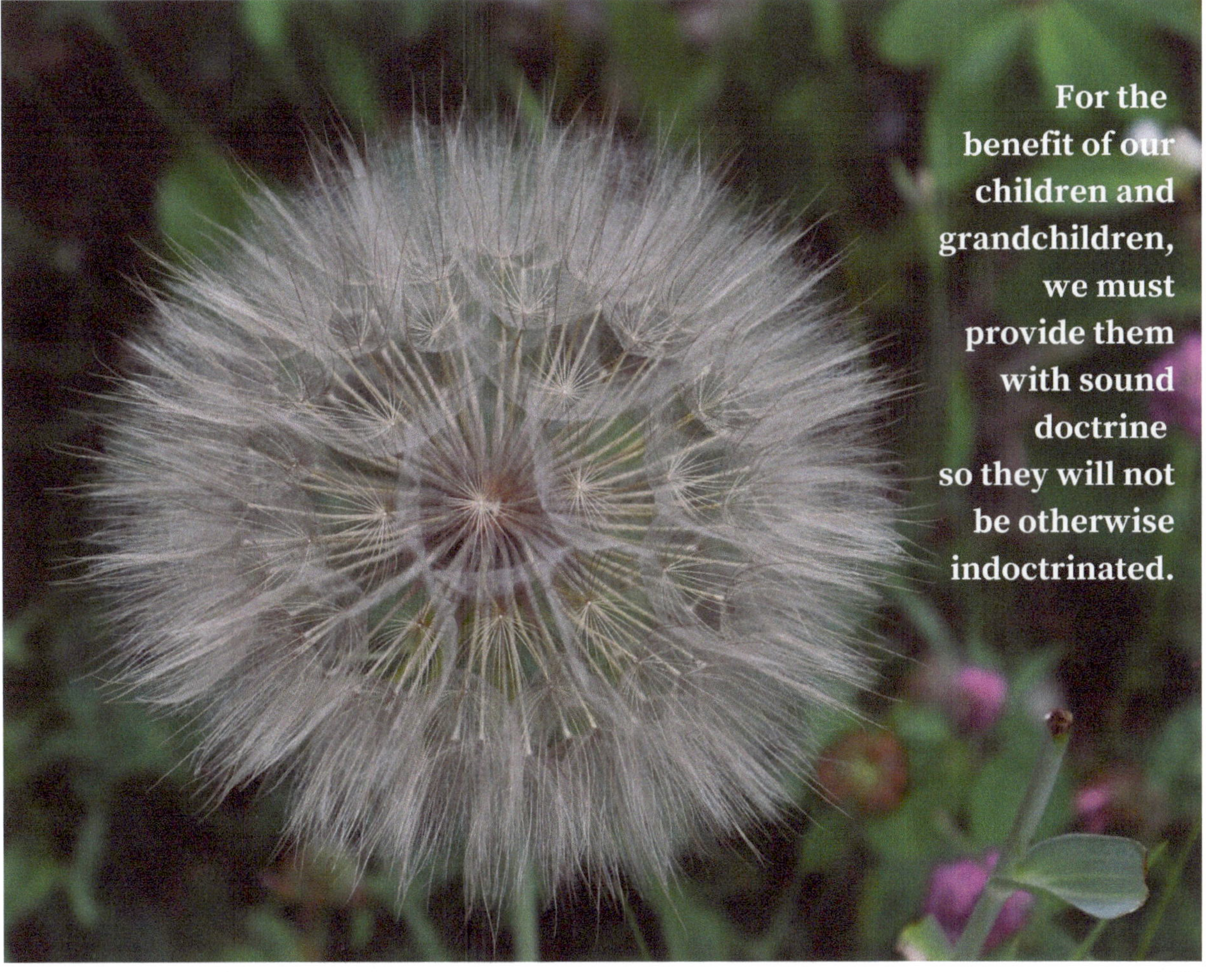
For the
benefit of our
children and
grandchildren,
we must
provide them
with sound
doctrine
so they will not
be otherwise
indoctrinated.

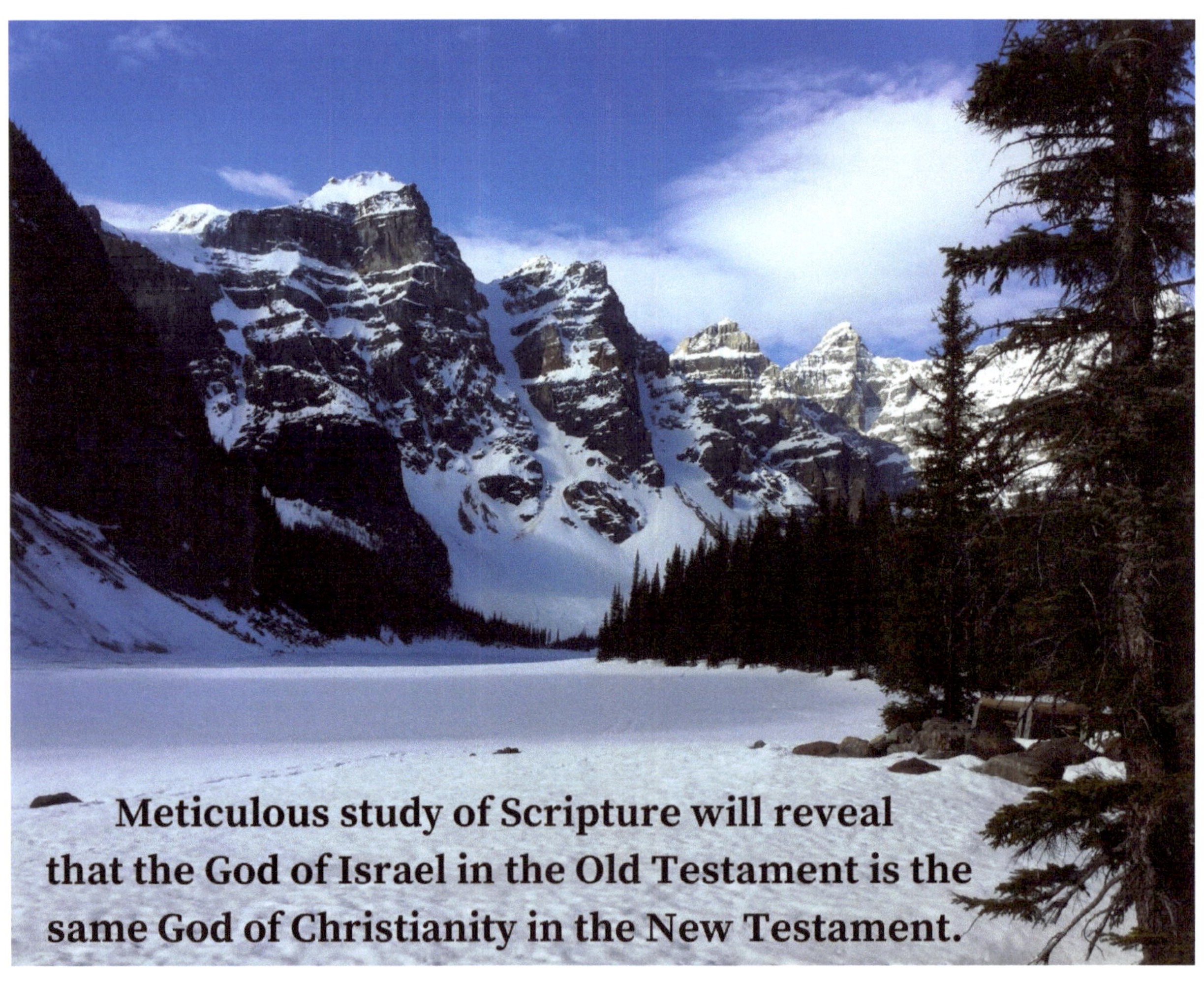

Moraine Lake in Spring – Banff National Park – Alberta

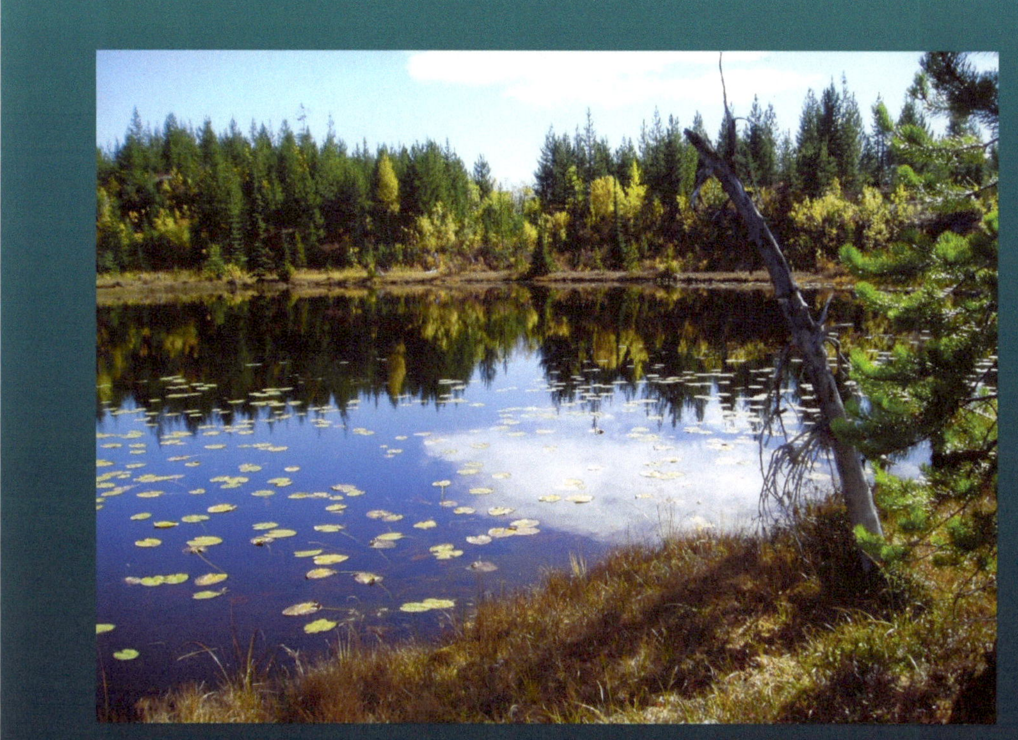

When "God gave them over to a debased mind," He caused them to lose reasoning ability. With no base, the mind has no foundation to be able to think and discern. Lack of reasoning ability and poor judgment ensue.

Jab Lake – Columbia Valley – British Columbia

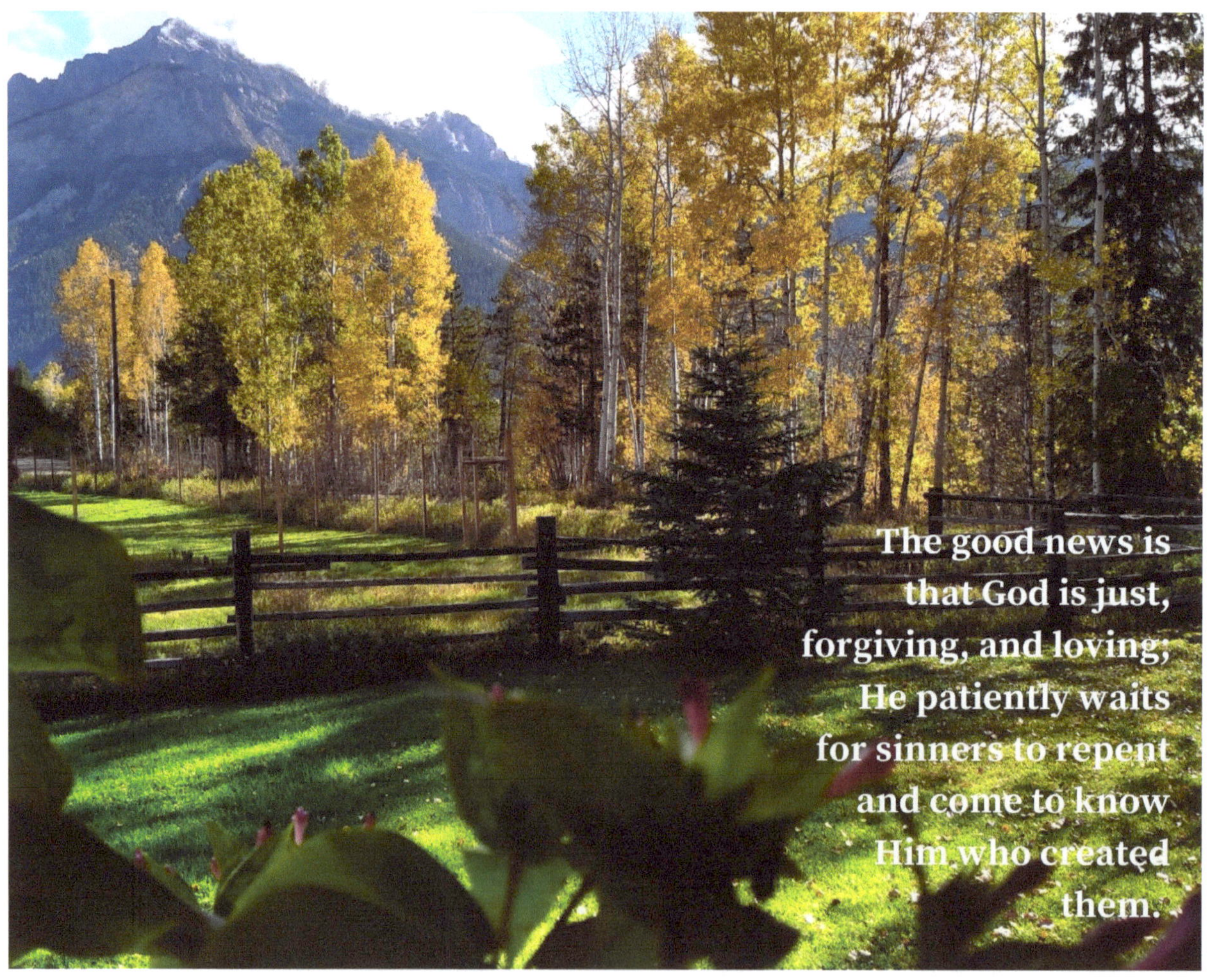

Fall in the Blaeberry Valley – British Columbia

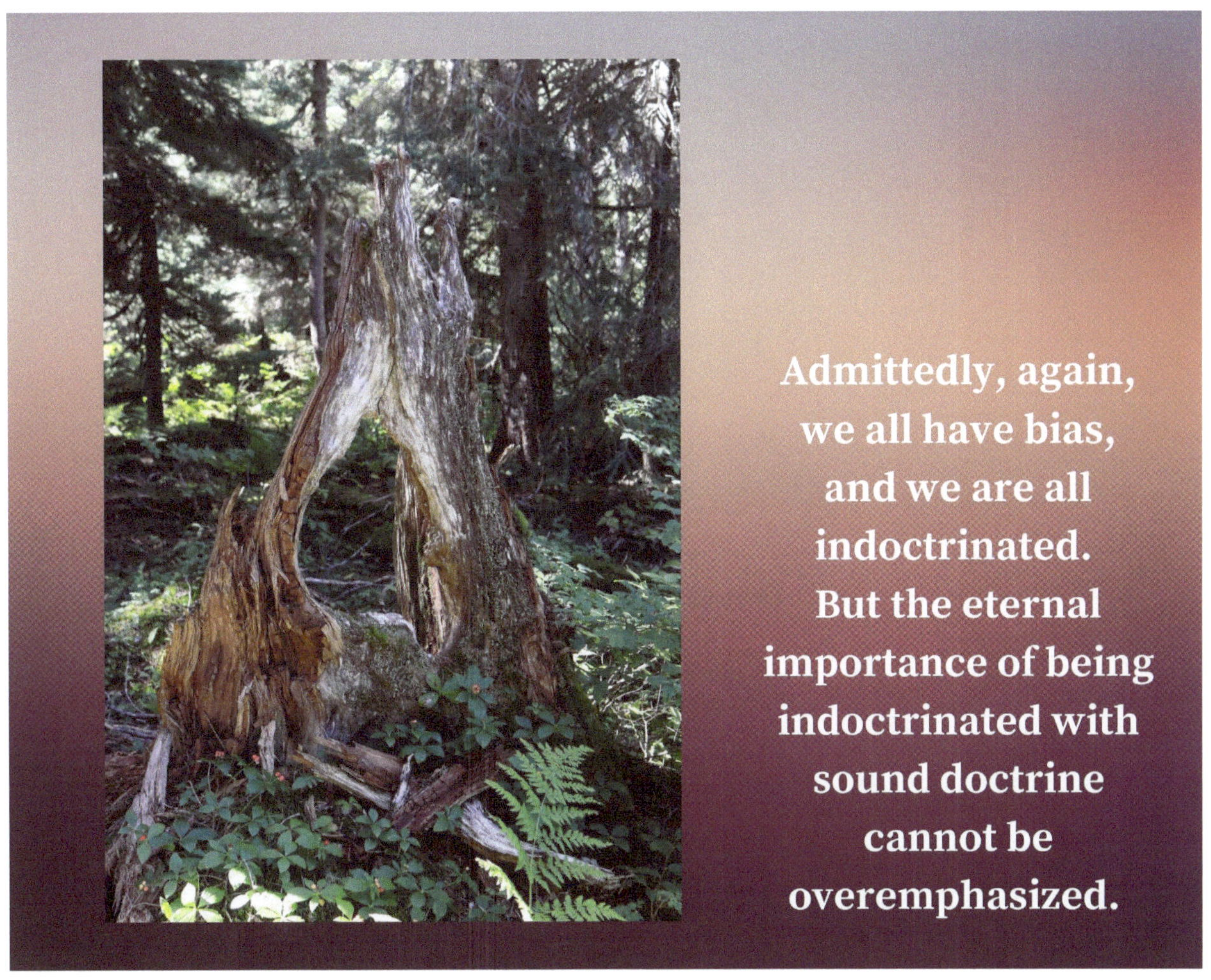

Admittedly, again,
we all have bias,
and we are all
indoctrinated.
But the eternal
importance of being
indoctrinated with
sound doctrine
cannot be
overemphasized.

Glacier Crest Trail – Glacier National Park – British Columbia

Unforeseen Future

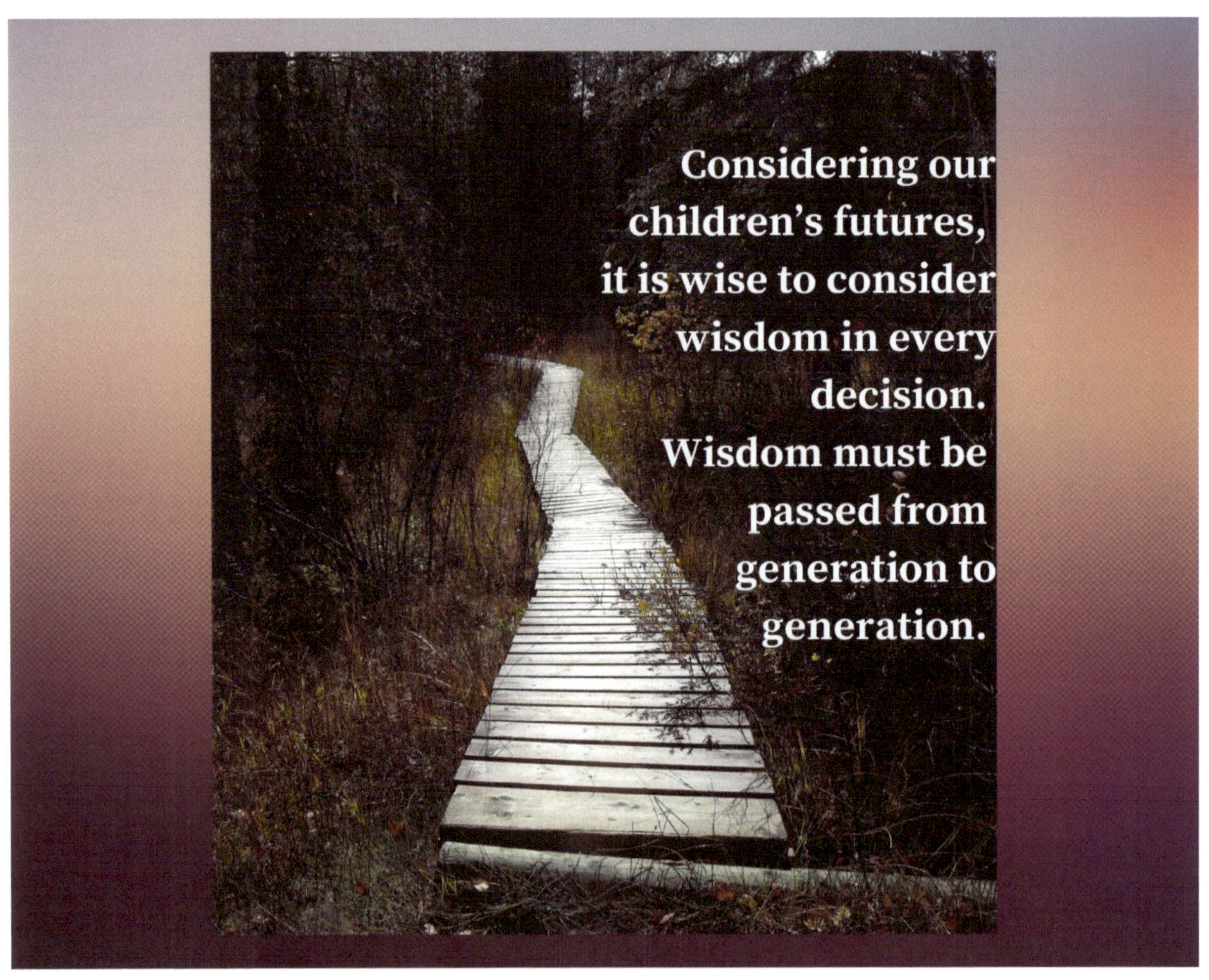

Blaeberry Valley – British Columbia

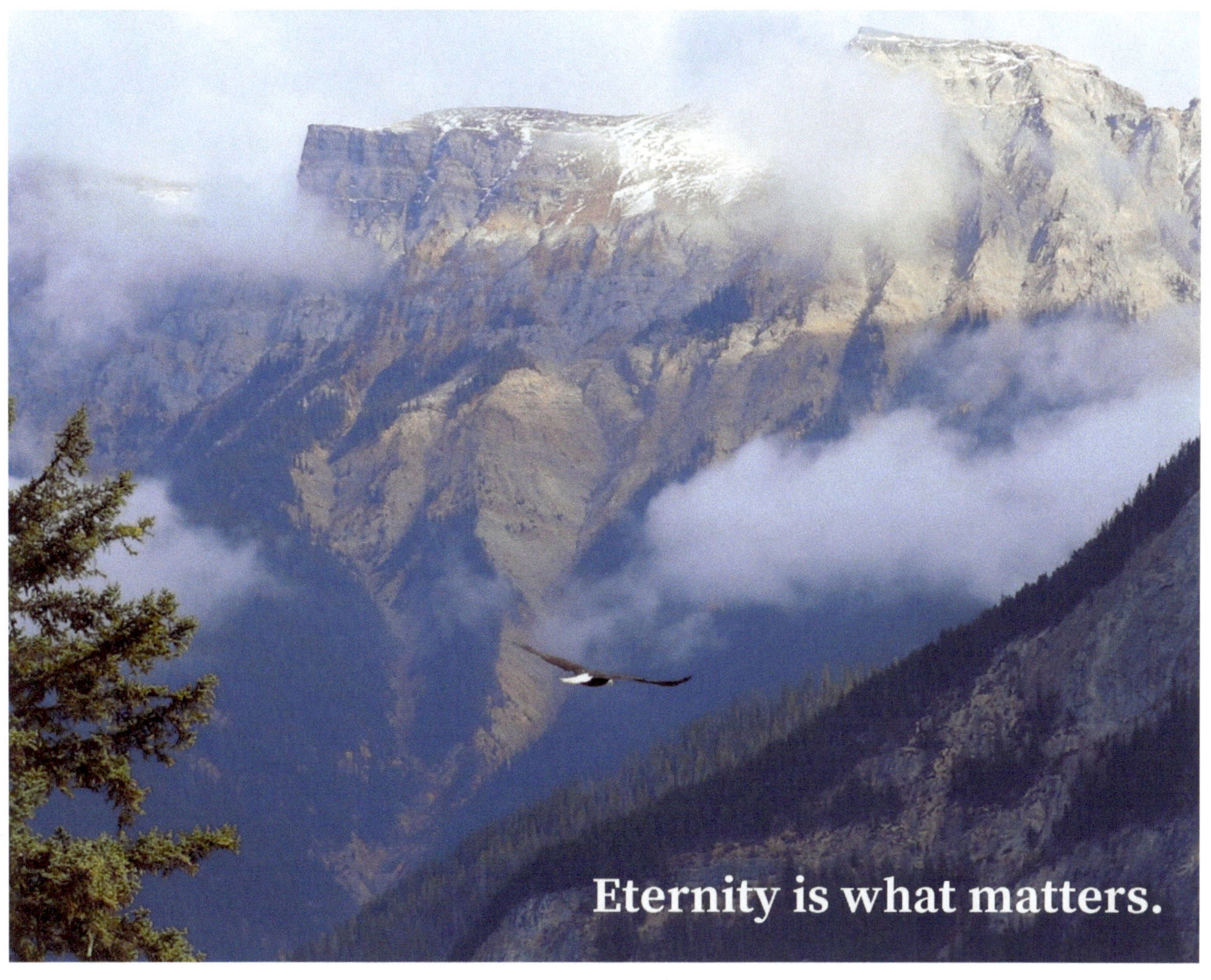

Bald Eagle with Redburn Mountain in Background – Blaeberry Valley – British Columbia

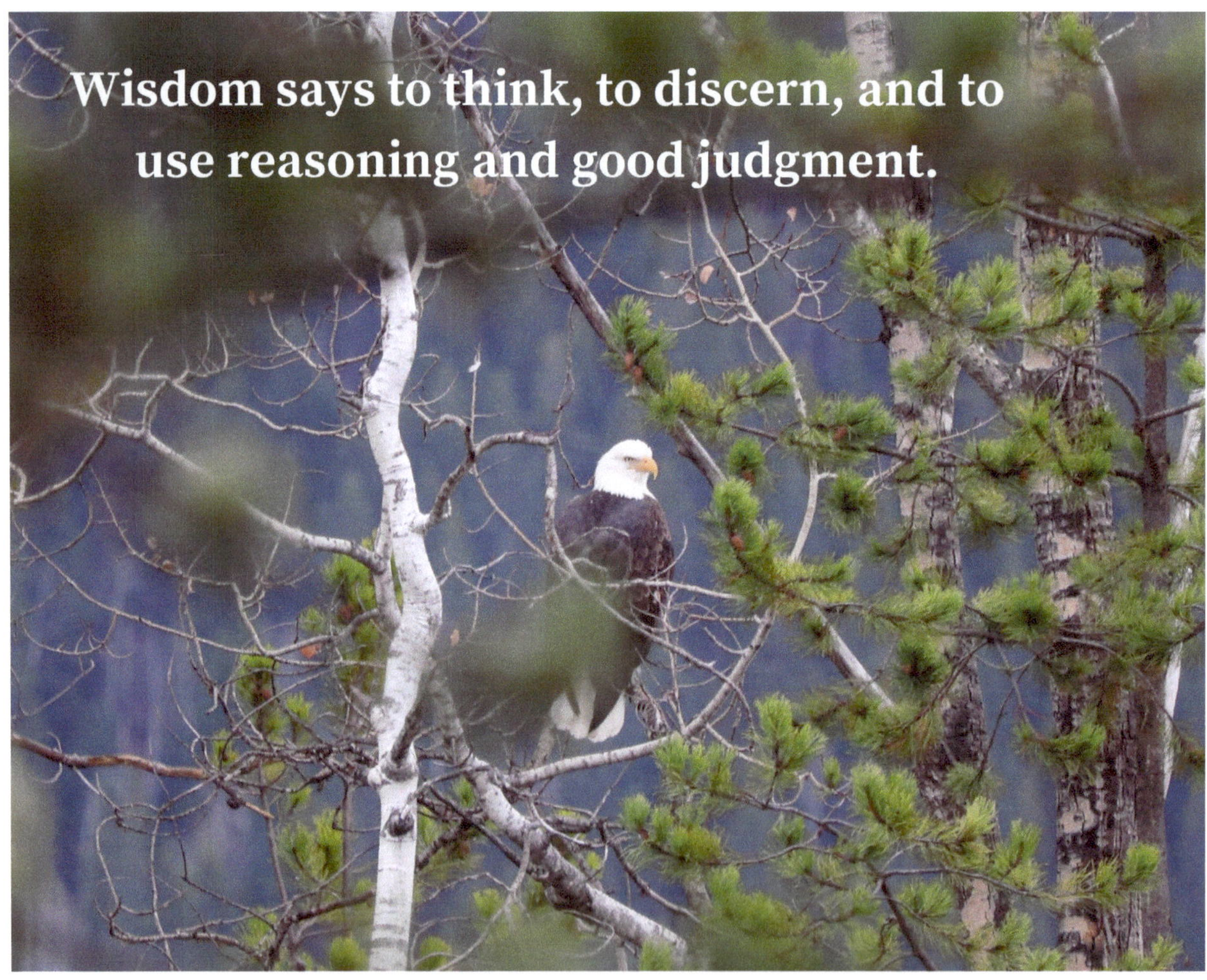

Bald Eagle – Blaeberry River – British Columbia

Forgive and Forget

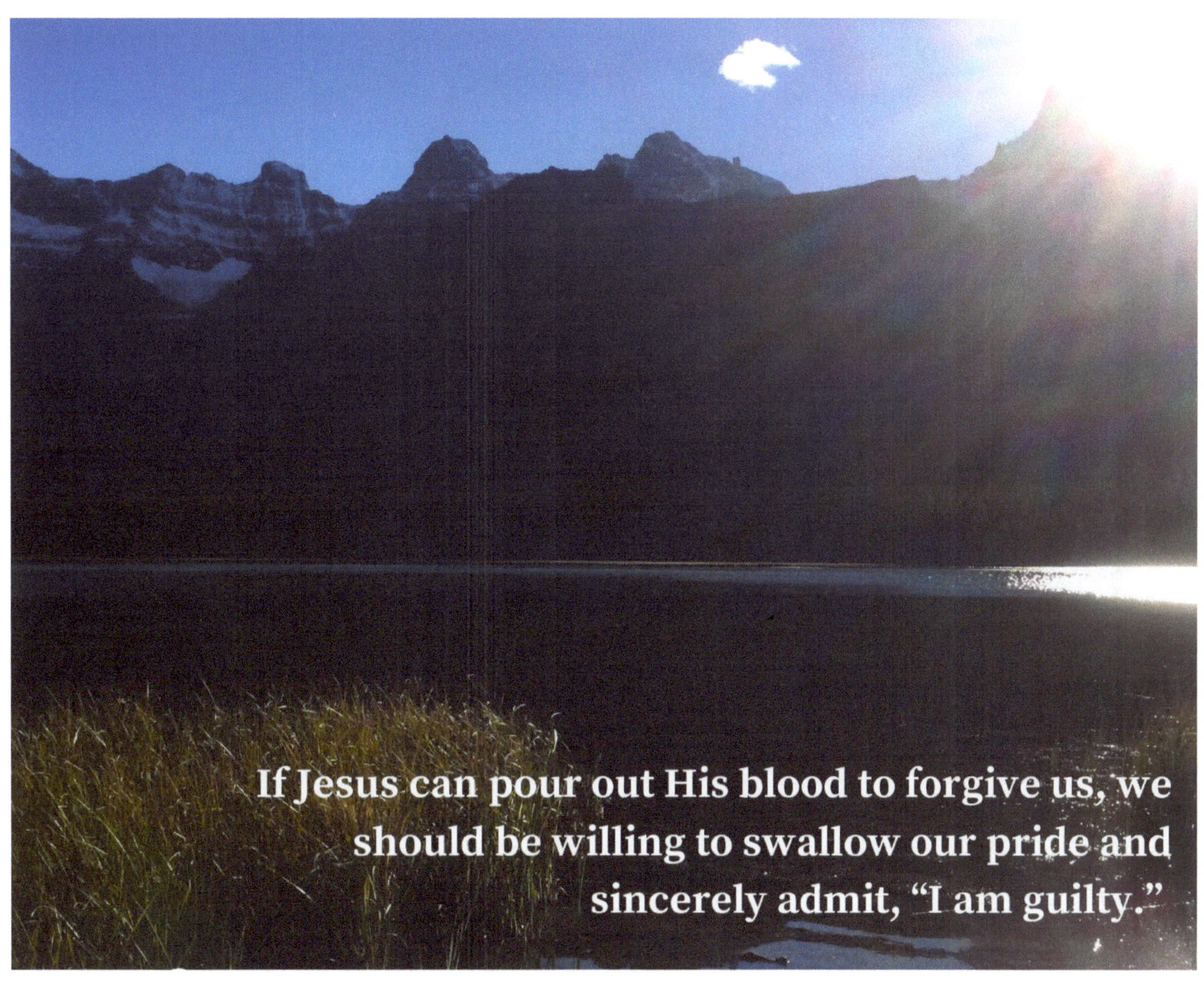

Moose Lake – Banff National Park – Alberta

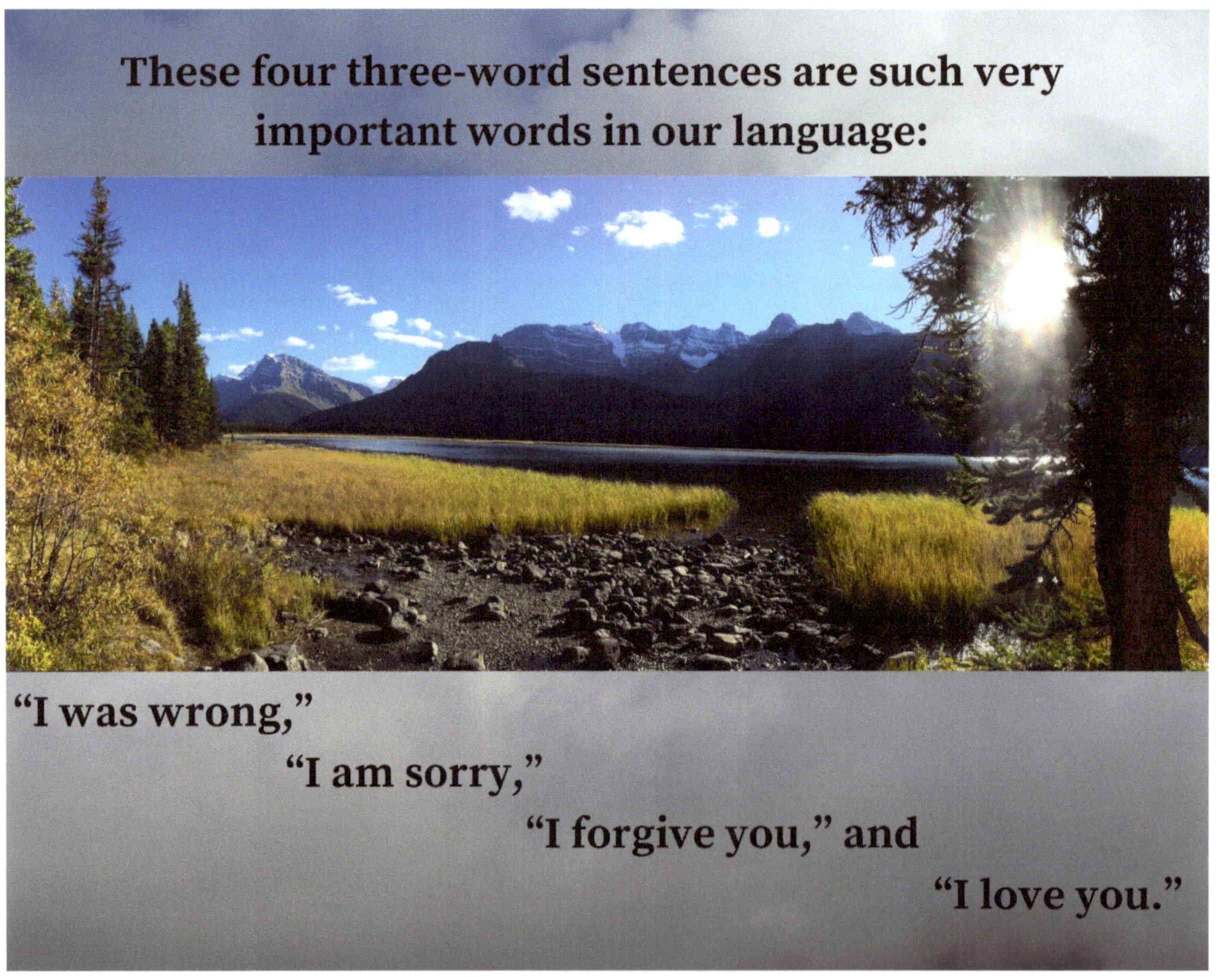

Moose Lake – Banff National Park – Alberta

Spiritual Warfare

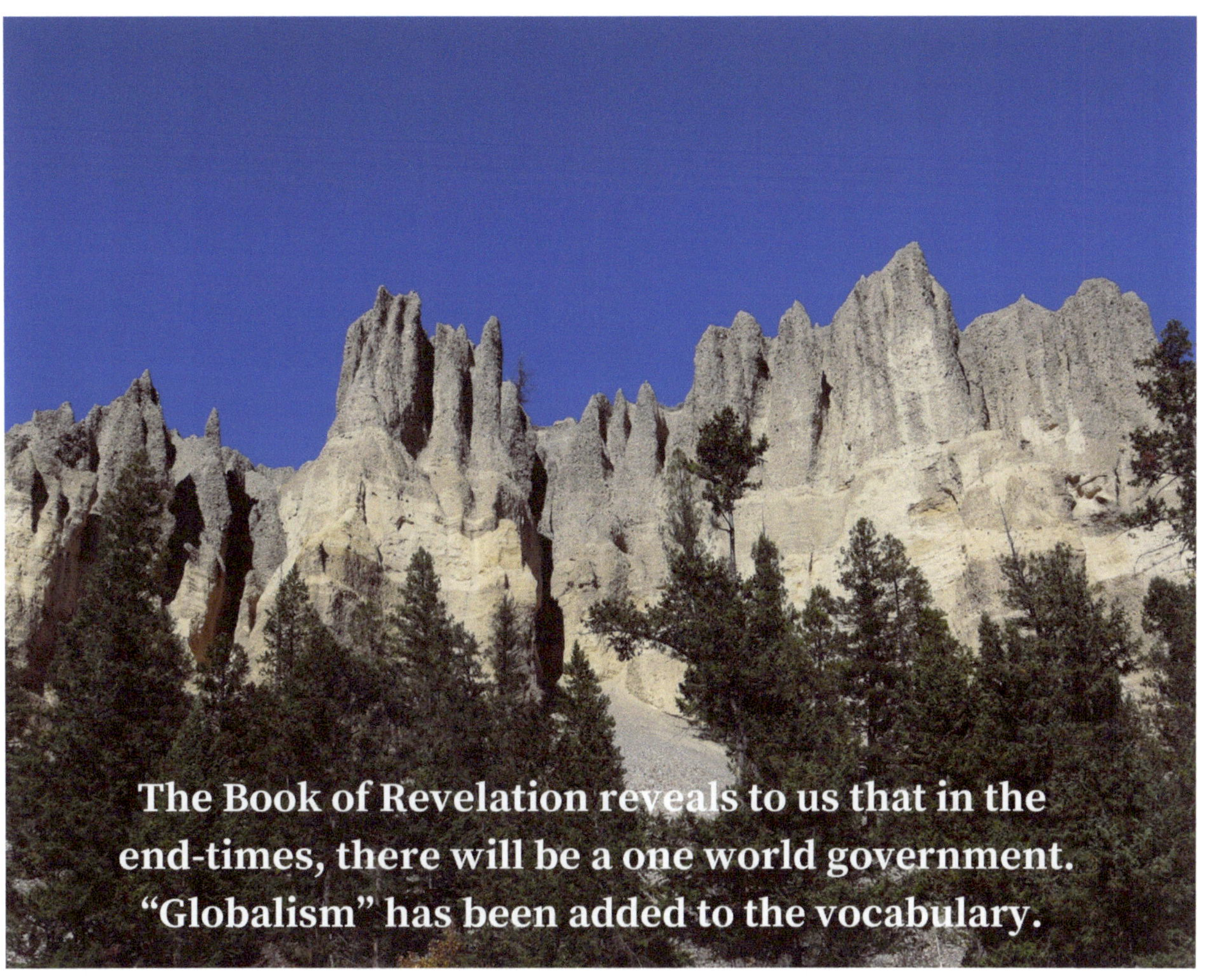

Hoodoos – Fairmont Hot Springs – British Columbia

If the doctrine of religions can be taught, it would make sense if the students could compare the key writings of Christianity to all the other religions. It would provide a more thorough education and would be fair to all.

Illecillewaet Glacier – Glacier Crest Trail – Glacier National Park – British Columbia

Delicate Issue

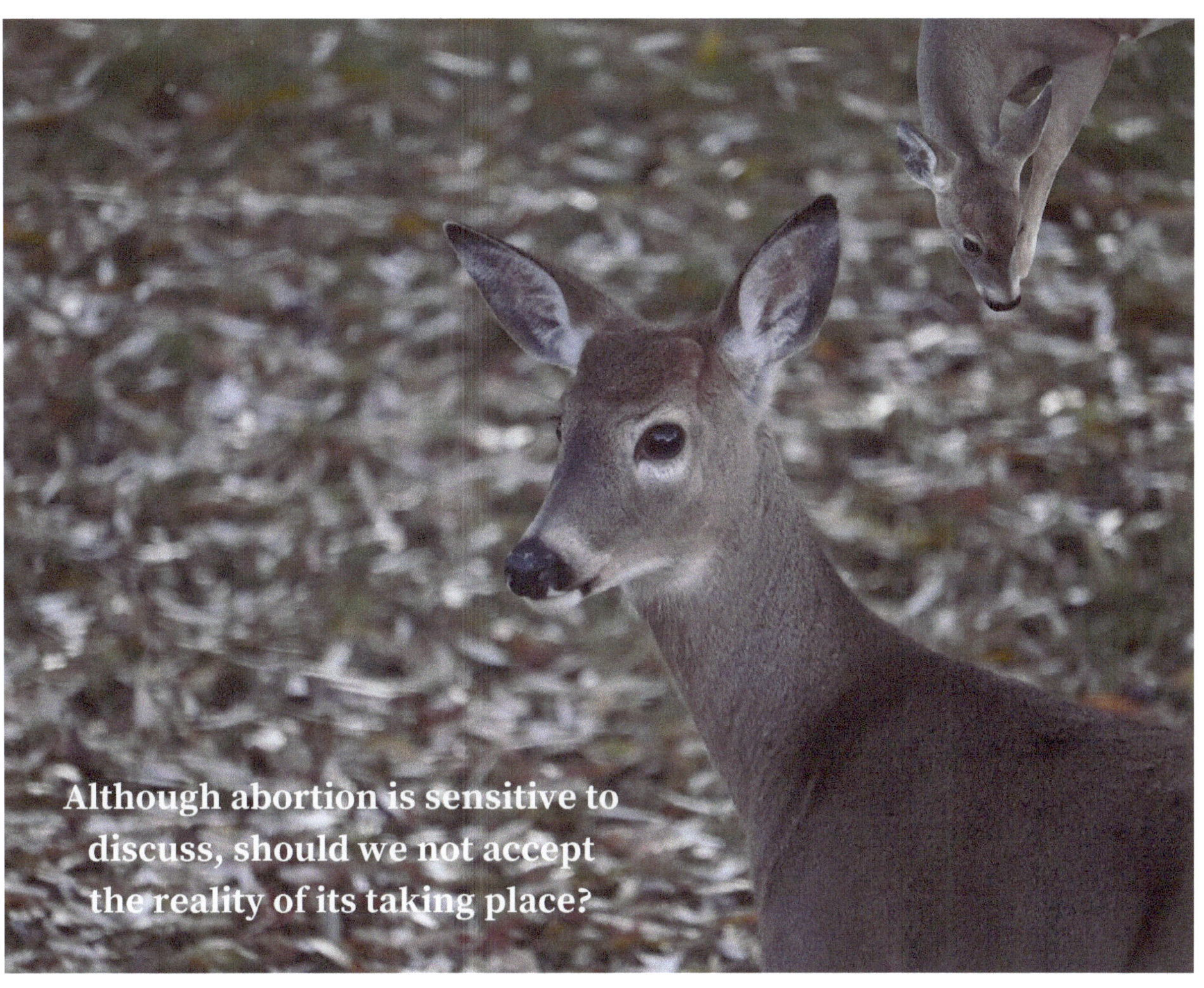

Whitetail Deer – Blaeberry Valley – British Columbia

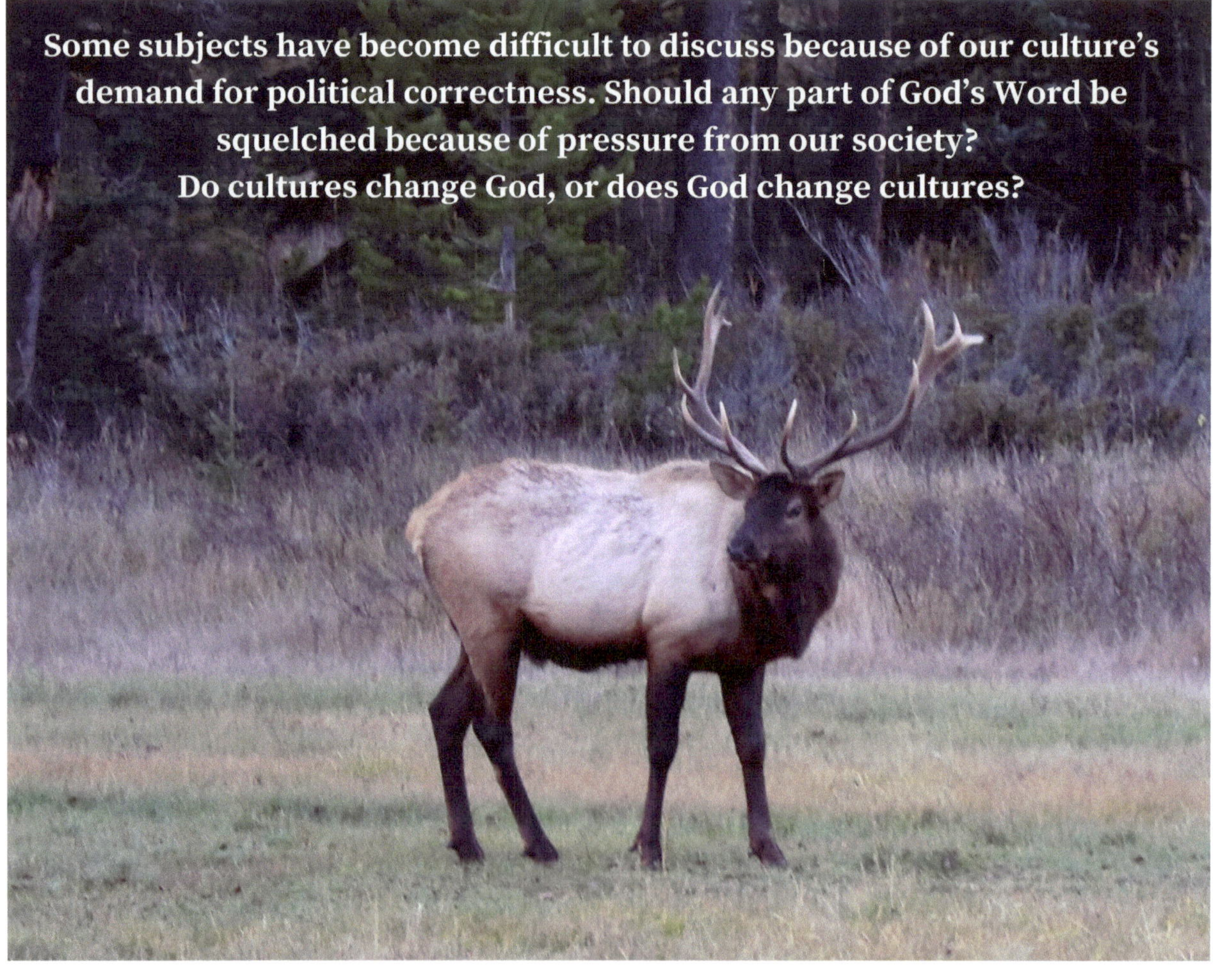

Bull Elk – Blaeberry Valley – British Columbia

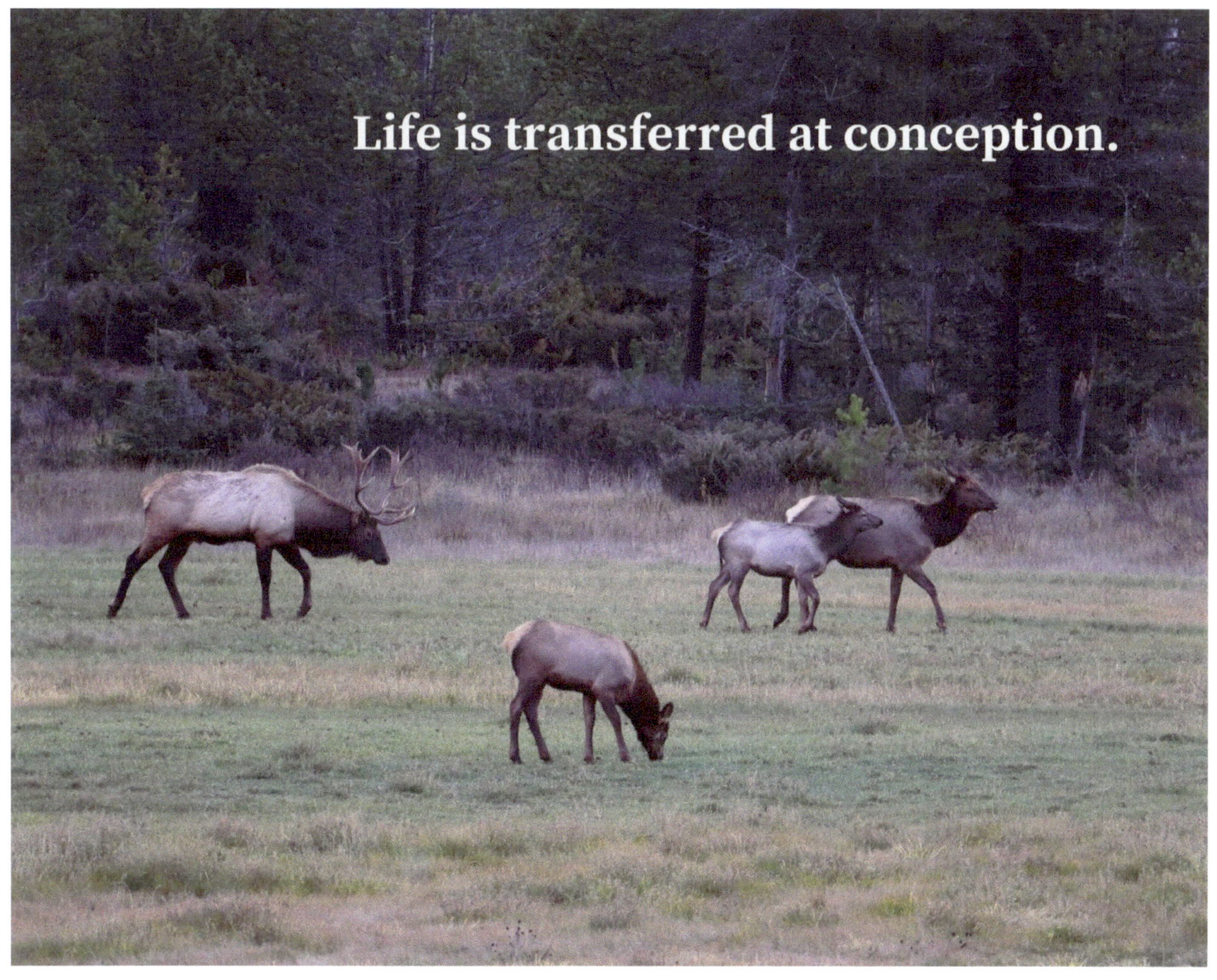

Elk Family – Blaeberry Valley – British Columbia

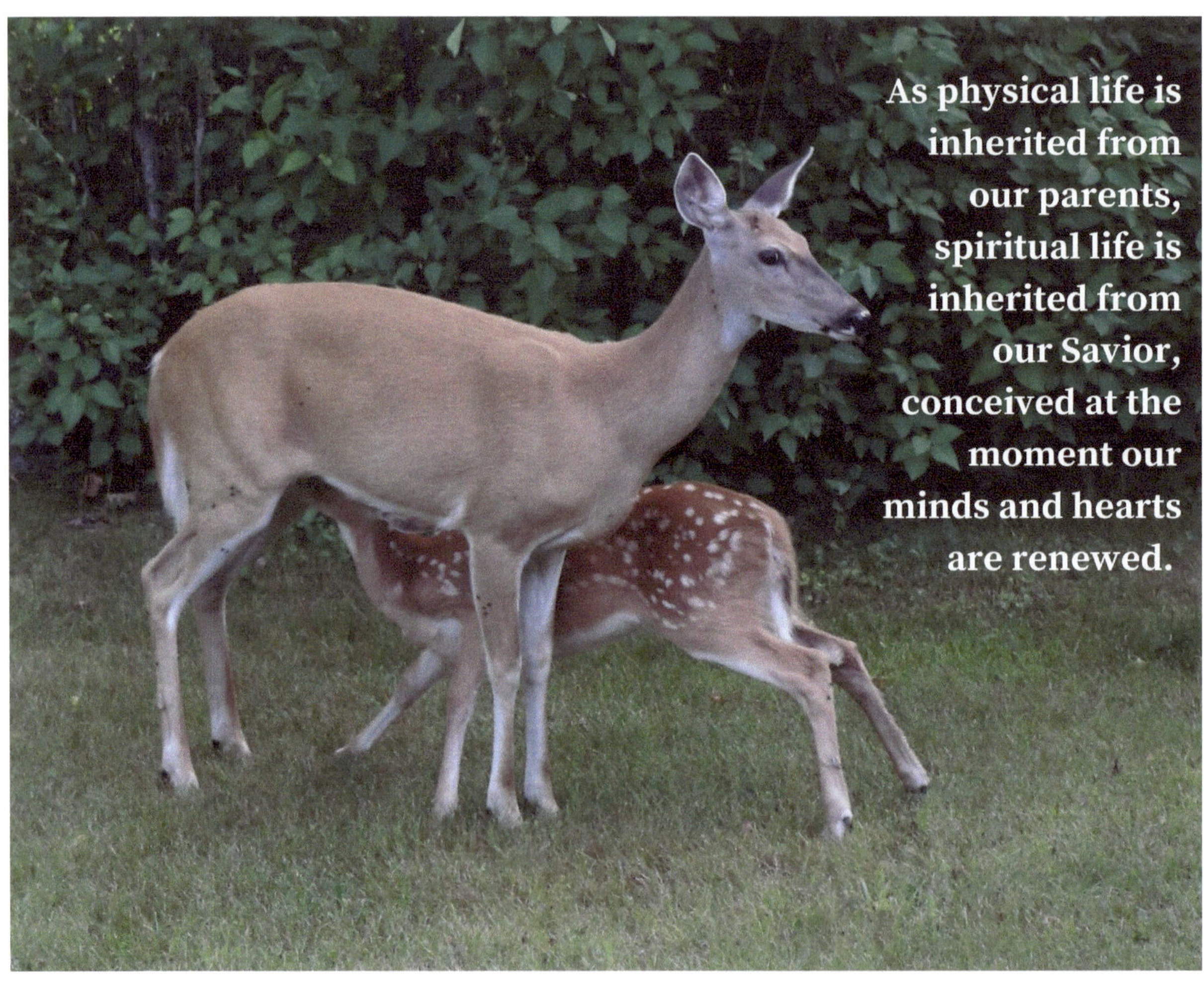

Doe with Fawn – Blaeberry Valley – British Columbia

Unrevised History

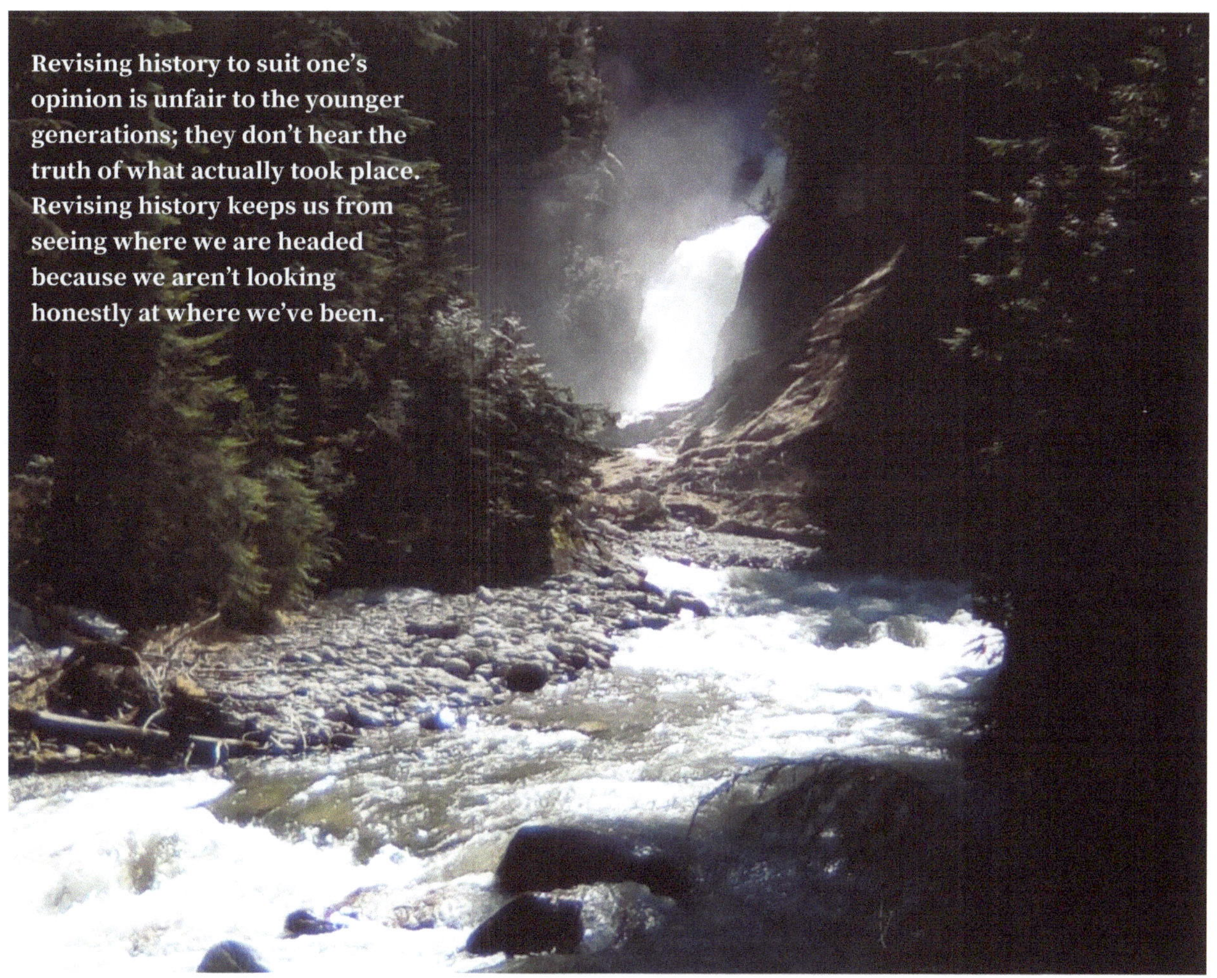

Bear Falls – Glacier National Park – British Columbia

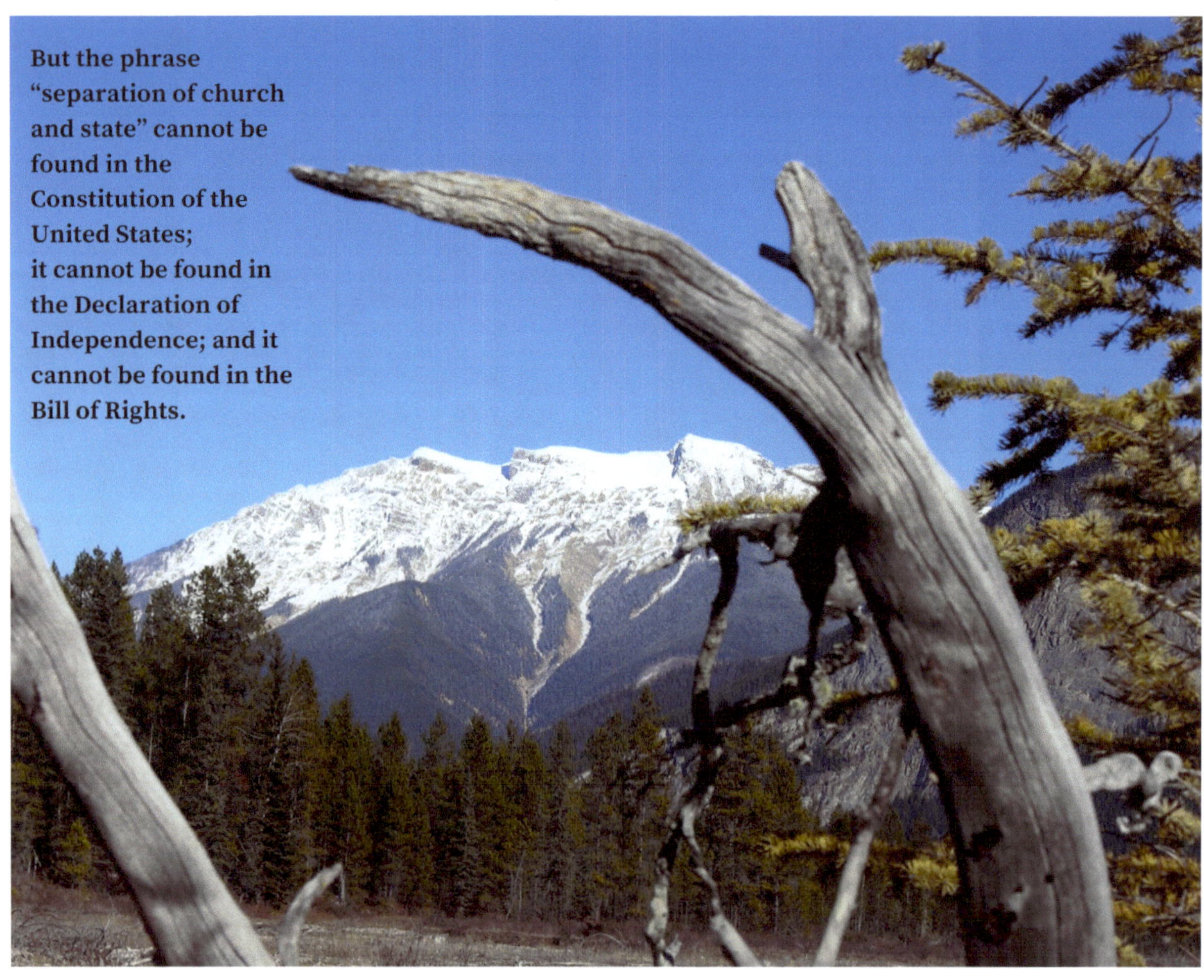

Redburn Mountain – Blaeberry River – British Columbia

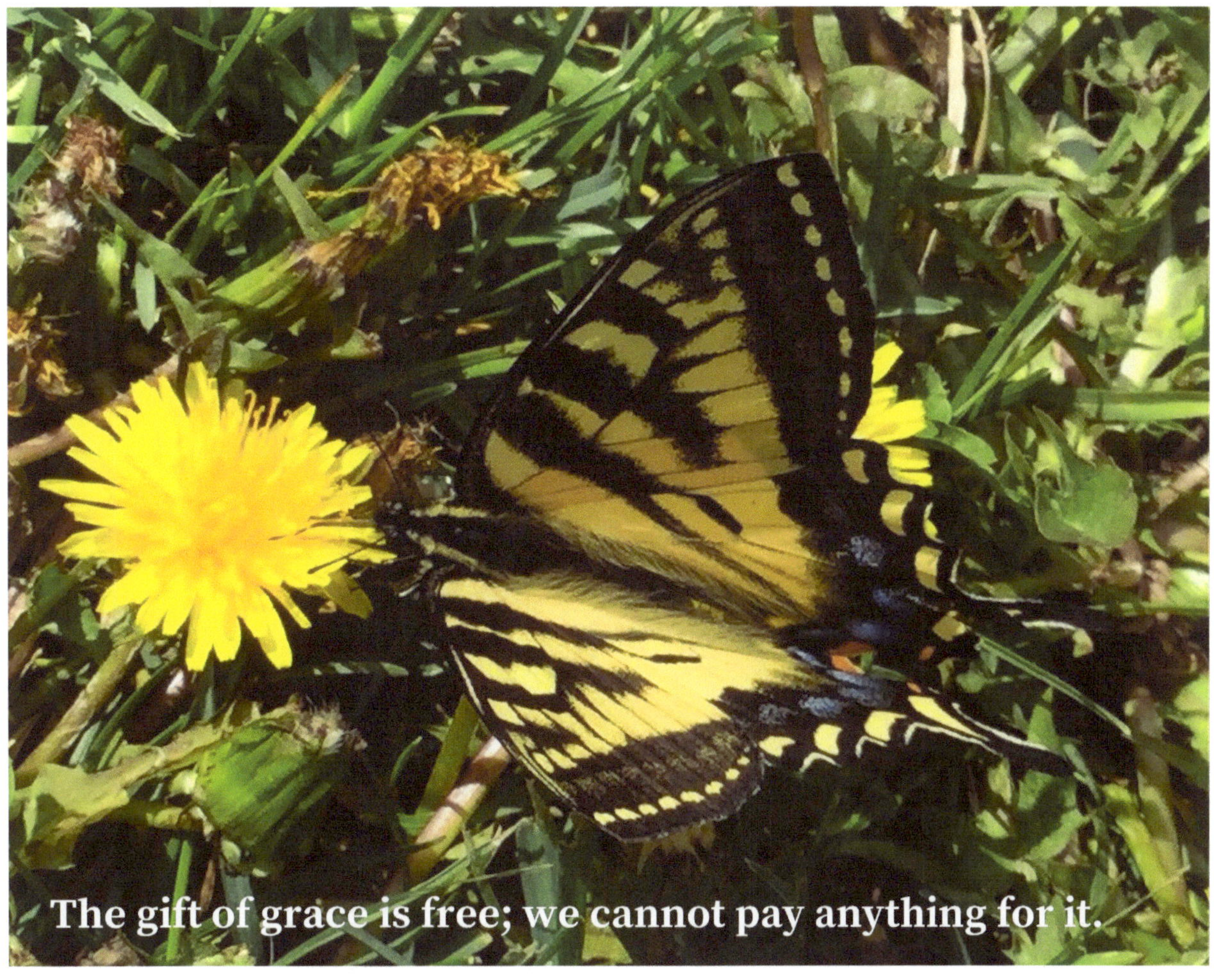

Tiger Swallowtail Butterfly – Blaeberry Valley – British Columbia

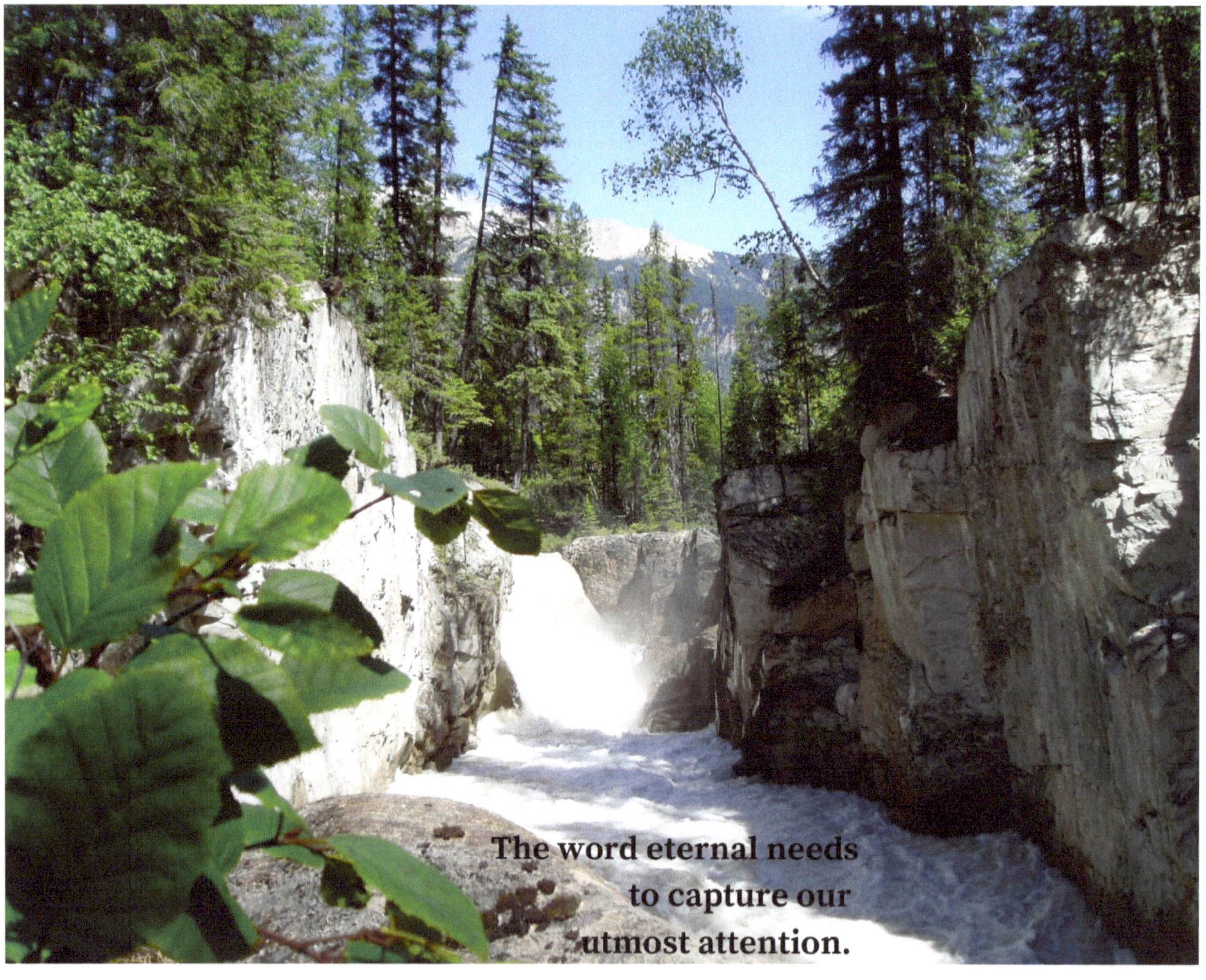

Thompson Falls – Blaeberry Valley – British Columbia

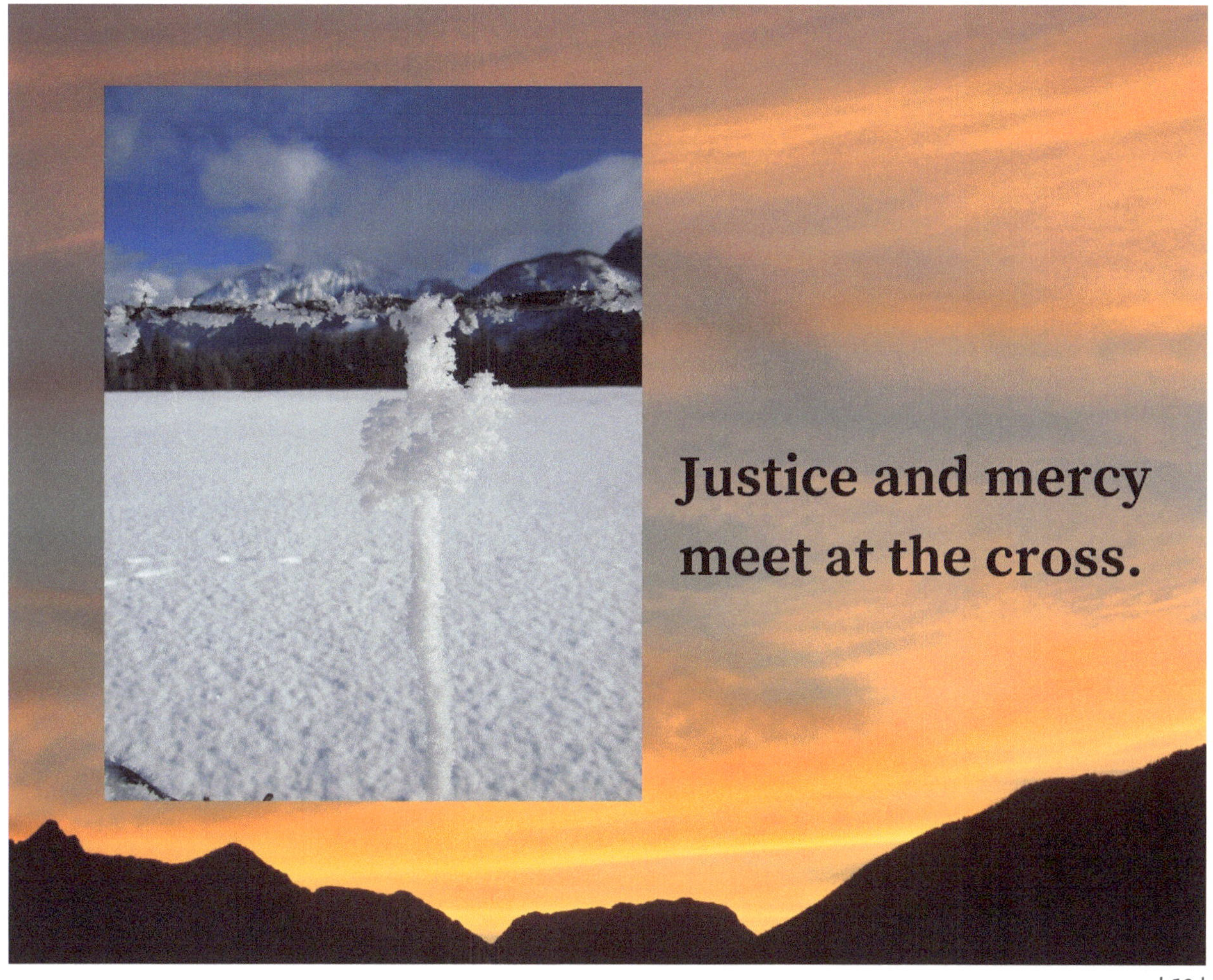

Justice and mercy meet at the cross.

Elfriede and her husband Michael Copple live in the Canadian Rocky Mountains. Their home is located in the heart of 6 National Parks. They are passionate about their faith and the Lord Jesus Christ. Together they author and publish Christian books.

The quotes in the photos were taken from the book "Considering Wisdom"

by Christian Author Michael Copple
ISBN 978-1-9736-9622-3 (sc)
ISBN 978-1-9736-9623-0 (hc)
ISBN 978-1-9736-9621-6 (e)

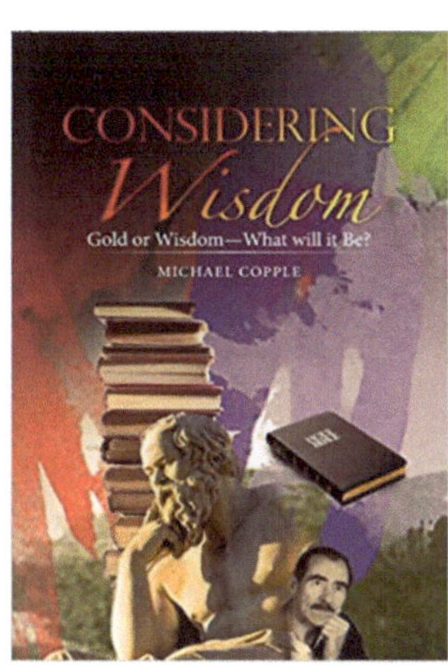

Check out Michael's Website/Blog at: https://michaelcopple.com/

Elfriede's Website/Blog at: https://holisticnutritionretreat.ca/

You can also reach Elfriede at: elfriedeandmike@gmail.com
and Mike at: mike@michaelcopple.com

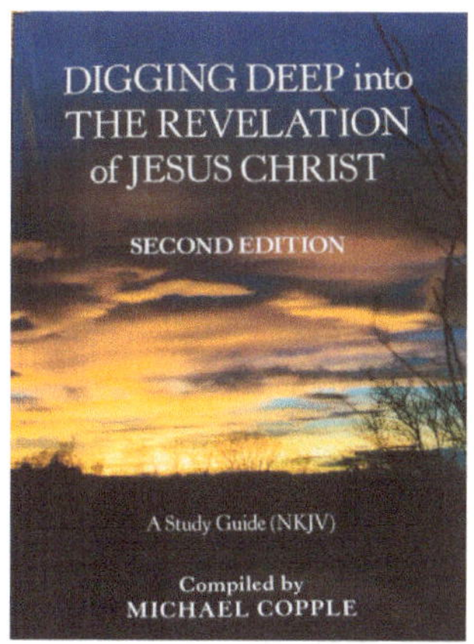

DIGGING DEEP into THE REVELATION OF JESUS CHRIST
A STUDY GUIDE (to the Book of Revelation)
ISBN 978-1-9736-4917-5 (sc)

EXAM BOOKLET to the Study Guide
DIGGING DEEP into THE REVELATION OF JESUS CHRIST
Questions-Answers-References
ISBN 978-1-7778325-1-3 (sc)
ISBN 978-1-7778325-0-6 (e)

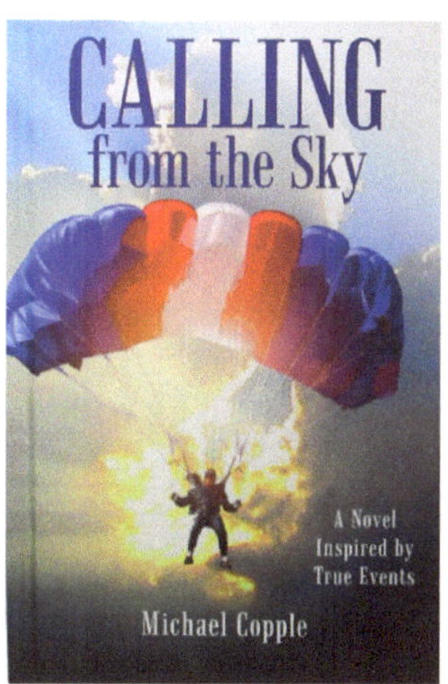

CALLING FROM THE SKY
A Novel inspired by True Events
ISBN 978-19736-6903-6 (sc)
ISBN 978-19736-6904-3 (hc)
ISBN 978-19736-6902-9 (e)

Check out Michael's Website/Blog at: https://michaelcopple.com/

www.ingramcontent.com/pod-product-compliance
Lightning Source LLC
Chambersburg PA
CBHW042114030726
47599CB00002B/213